Exploring DARTMOOR AGAIN

EXPLORATION MADE EASY

Harry Starkey

Revised, updated and illustrated by
George Thurlow

Peninsula Press

Published by Peninsula Press Ltd
P.O. Box 31
Newton Abbot
Devon
TQ12 5XH

Telephone and Fax: 01803 875875

First published 1981 by F.H. Starkey
Reprinted 1983, 1986
Revised and updated edition 1998

Printed in England by
The Cromwell Press, Melksham, Wiltshire.

ISBN 1 872640 42 7

By the same author: Exploring Dartmoor (Revised and updated edition 1995)
Dartmoor – Then and Now (1986)
Odds and Ends from Dartmoor (1984)
Dartmoor Crosses and Some Ancient Tracks (1983)

CONTENTS

PREFACE

The success of *Exploring Dartmoor,* Harry Starkey's first book of walks, was such that his friends found it easier to persuade him to write a second one. Having finished it he had some difficulty in deciding on a suitable title and eventually settled on *Exploring Dartmoor Again.*

Harry Starkey loved and knew Dartmoor and could always suggest a fresh aspect to stimulate walkers seeking a route and explain what could be seen on the way. He delighted in sharing the thrill of roaming the open moor, revelling in its natural beauty and exploring evidence of history and prehistory with anyone who would enjoy it. That is what he did in this book.

Aware that some changes have inevitably arisen since Harry Starkey first researched these walks the publishers have sought advice from the Dartmoor National Park Authority in producing this fully revised edition.

George Thurlow has generously illustrated the walks and revised the route descriptions so that the reader can be confident that it remains a readable guide for anyone exploring Dartmoor for the first time or, indeed, exploring Dartmoor again.

John Starkey, 1998

MAP OF DARTMOOR

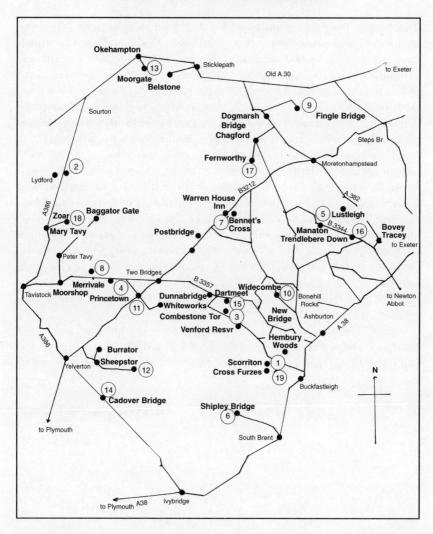

PLEASE NOTE: This map is diagramatic only. Its main purpose is to help the explorer find routes and starting places. It is not intended and should not be used as a substitute for a proper map. In some cases to do so might even be dangerous. See page 10 for information about Ordnance Survey maps. The numbered circles indicate the approximate starting places for the Explorations whose numbers appear in the circles.

The map is on a scale of approximately one inch to one mile.

FOREWORD to 1981 Edition

This book is published in the hope that it will supplement and continue the exploration of Dartmoor begun in my first book, *Exploring Dartmoor*, which came out in 1980. Apart from some of the material in the introductory chapter, very little of the information about specific places, tracks and areas contained in this book appeared in the first. All the explorations are new. This being so, the book is just as suitable for people who are newly beginning to discover the delights and fascination of Dartmoor as its forerunner. In other words, the two books can be used separately or together – they complement one another.

My own qualifications to write such a book as this are summed up in the following extract from the Foreword to *Exploring Dartmoor*: "…we came to live in Devon in 1965. To be near Dartmoor we settled at Haytor Vale and from this vantage point I have continued and intensified the exploration of the Moor that I had already started. For several years past I have been lecturing about Dartmoor for the Workers' Educational Association – there is a great and continuously growing interest in the subject – and many friends have pressed me to commit to writing what I have said to them in my talks. I have been reluctant to do this because I have always felt that there are many people better qualified to do so than I, but at last I have succumbed to pressure and what follows is the result…".

Finally, it is nearly thirty years since I first began my love affair with Dartmoor. I hope that all readers of this book will derive as much pleasure, joy and interest from their contact with the Moor as I have – I count it as one of the great blessings of my life.

F.H. Starkey (writing in 1981)

INTRODUCTION

Readers of my previous book *Exploring Dartmoor,* will recognise in this introductory chapter much with which they are familiar. I must crave their indulgence however, for the information herein contained is vital if readers of this book who are not familiar with the earlier one are to enjoy their days on Dartmoor in comfort and safety and with a reasonable appreciation of the obligations of an explorer to those whose business and livelihood lie upon the Moor.

First, as to the area that this book sets out to explore. Dartmoor is a word which, if loosely applied, can be misleading. For the purpose of this book then the word means the high, semi-mountainous area of Devon which centres about the Forest of Dartmoor,* including the vast unfenced commons which lie around the forest. Most of the area stands at an altitude of 1000 feet or more above sea level and by far the greater part of it lies within the Dartmoor National Park.

The phrase "Dartmoor National Park" causes a good deal of misunderstanding and demands a little explanation. The National Park came into existence in 1951 under the authority of Parliament.

It covers an area of 360 square miles, including the great majority of the high moorland surrounding the Forest of Dartmoor and the Forest itself, plus some beautiful country around the perimeter at a lower altitude, especially in the valley of the River Teign on the eastern side. Most of the countryside in the National Park, including the unfenced commons and moorland, is privately owned. This of course includes the hundreds of farms, fields, woodlands, rivers, streams and villages. There are numerous public rights of way, i.e. public footpaths and bridle paths and wide expanses of common and moorland over which the public right of access is never disputed.

On central Dartmoor, within the Forest, are several immense enclosed areas totalling thousands of acres known as newtakes. These enclosures were made

---

* As he or she proceeds, the reader of the book will come across frequent references to "The Forest of Dartmoor" and "the Forest". This will inevitably give rise to the question "why call it a forest when there are so few trees on Dartmoor?" This is not the place to enter into a lengthy dissertation about a subject so complex as this, but briefly the explanation is as follows. The central 75 square miles or so of the upland area that we call Dartmoor is part and parcel of the Duchy of Cornwall and has been for many centuries. In former times this area was a royal hunting ground and as such was called a forest, from the Latin word *foris*. The amount of woodland in the area has no bearing upon its status as a Royal Forest, though it seems likely that there were more trees on Dartmoor in the early days than is now the case – leaving aside the modern conifer plantations, that is.The boundaries of the Forest were fixed in the 13th century and are much the same today as they were then.

in the 18th/19th centuries when much of Dartmoor was being "improved". Most belong to the Duchy of Cornwall and are let to various tenants for grazing purposes. Over recent years public access to many of these areas has been put on a formal basis through the negotiation of access agreements; some agreements may provide access to the whole of the particular newtake, others provide access by virtue of permitted paths. It must be remembered that the people who rent the newtakes also have rights and every care should be taken not to disturb the livestock within them, whether ponies, cattle or sheep. Great care must also be taken not to damage walls, etc. and to shut gates after use.

As will be explained later, large sections of northern Dartmoor are used as live firing ranges by the military authorities. Some of these ranges extend into the newtakes. When this happens access to the ranges is curtailed whilst firing takes place.

The Dartmoor National Park Authority is a statutory body which has a duty to conserve and enhance Dartmoor's natural beauty and cultural heritage, and to promote the enjoyment and understanding of the area's special qualities. To achieve this the Authority works very closely with a wide range of different landowners. Ever since the National Park was founded controversy has raged about the sanctity of the Park. Although fewer than 50 years have gone by since its foundation, already there are to be seen many new signs of the march of "progress" – reservoirs, commercial afforestation, wire fences dividing up the newtakes, military misuse and the rest. This is to say nothing of the damage done to the surface of the Moor by tens of thousands of human feet, and its priceless relics of man's 4000 years of occupation suffer likewise.

Those whose duty and responsibility it is to manage the National Park have a difficult if not impossible task in reconciling the various interests involved – progress with conservation; agriculture with amenity; the concept of a National Park with a permanent military presence which includes live firing. All these add up to a fearful paradox likely to daunt Solomon himself. The problem is not made easier by the fact that many intelligent people do not believe and will not accept that wild moorland country has a beauty and value of its own. They cannot grasp that a beautiful valley is not made more beautiful by flooding it with water and that to add a great wall of concrete to hold back the water is more likely to ruin than enhance the beauty. Many people also do not understand that "improvement" frequently destroys beauty with no compensating gain to anyone but the improver. Only time will tell, but I am sure in my own mind as I can be of anything that the one thing that should happen to Dartmoor is that it should be conserved. As the pace of life becomes more and more hectic and as noise and polution creep into every crack and crevice of our national life, so will the peace and solitude of the few areas of wild country left in Britain become more and more valuable. Let us treasure what we have – if we lose it it will be gone for ever.

Before beginning the physical exploration of any area, it is advisable to do some reading about it and have a look at a map of the area; the larger the scale of the map the better.

There are scores, yes hundreds, of books about Dartmoor of all shapes, sizes and degrees of usefulness. The Moor has been described and discussed time and time again by authors of all periods from the 17th century to the present day. The history of the Royal and Ancient Forest of Dartmoor and of the Commons of Devon which abut upon the Forest has been pondered over and conjectured about by learned people. So have the origins of the numerous prehistoric remains to be found on the Moor and the interpretation to be placed upon them. The same is true of the ancient dwarfed oakwoods; the tinners' remains; the origins of the tors and every other aspect of this extraordinarily interesting area that one can think of.

Despite all that has been written and said about Dartmoor, only one person, in my opinion, has ever produced a truly comprehensive guide-book to the Moor. That person was William Crossing, who died in 1928 at the age of 81, having spent almost the whole of his active life in exploring Dartmoor and collecting information about it. His *Guide to Dartmoor* was first published in 1909 and, happily, is still available with a modern preface by Brian Le Messurier. The *Guide* is almost as correct and almost as valuable today as it was 90 years ago. But much has changed upon Dartmoor since Crossing's day and much has come to light that he could not have known about or that he did not describe because he was standing too close to the canvas.

It is hoped that this book will in some small measure serve to amplify Crossing's great work. Not that it sets out to supersede the *Guide*; there are few alive or indeed who have ever lived qualified to displace Crossing – I certainly am not one of them. What I hope to do is to describe in some detail a few areas of Dartmoor that I find of particular interest and which can be reached by ordinary people who do not want to walk more than a few miles but who do want to achieve the "sense of wonder" that is the true impelling force of the explorer and which comes from discovering and beginning to understand the previously unknown. At this stage it should be said that the excursions in this book are, on the whole, somewhat longer than those in the first.

If I were to begin a new exploration of Dartmoor tomorrow, there are four books that I would consider essential. These are:

Guide to Dartmoor by William Crossing (Peninsula Press),
Dartmoor by Richard Hansford Worth (Peninsula Press),
The Industrial Archaeology of Dartmoor by Helen Harris (Peninsula Press),
and *Prehistoric Dartmoor* by Paul Pettit (Forest Publishing).

With these one can make do or from them go on to some or all of the scores of others, all useful but some more so.

As to maps, we are well served. The Ordnance Survey publishes the *Tourist Map of Dartmoor* (scale 1 inch to 1 mile), which covers not only the National Park but also a large area around its perimeter and this is essential to all explorers of the Moor. For really detailed exploration the O.S. Outdoor Leisure Map No. 28 is ideal. At a scale of 1/25000 (about $2^1/_2$ inches to the mile) it covers the whole of Dartmoor on one sheet, and shows all public access land, registered footpaths and bridlepaths and an astonishing wealth of other detail. Everyone should learn to read a map and to use a compass. Information about this and about how to fix a six-figure map reference is to be found on all O.S maps.

A few last words in preparation and we will set out upon our first expedition. What do we need to do before we start?

Weather: Check the weather forecast and if it is not favourable do not venture out of sight of a road – you can still have a worthwhile expedition if you consult your map and choose an interesting area.

Equipment: Warm waterproof clothing and stout comfortable walking boots and thick socks – thick enough to prevent your feet from sliding about in your boots. Shoes are not really suitable except for short walks over dry terrain, nor are wellington boots although some people say they prefer them. Haversack or rucksack containing sandwiches, thermos, spare dry socks and spare pullover. Iron rations – chocolate, etc. Simple first aid items. Personally I always carry a whistle and a large white handkerchief – the human voice does not carry very well in the vastness of Dartmoor.

Maps and Compass: Make sure you have your map with you, and that your compass is working.

Where are we going? Decide in advance what area you are going to explore and which is your jumping off spot. Study the map for items of interest to visit. Tell someone where you intend to go to and what time you hope to return.

Parking: As to parking, please do be careful about this. The information given is accurate at the time of going to press but circumstances alter cases and a badly parked vehicle, left for hours on end, can engender much unnecessary ill-will. Do not leave valuables in your car, and ensure that it is locked.

Once started walking do not hurry but try to maintain a steady pace. If you achieve an average of two miles an hour on Dartmoor you will be doing well. If you are truly exploring, it will be much less than this. Use the best, i.e. the driest and smoothest ground available. Avoid very wet and rocky areas if possible, even if this means making a detour. (Motto – on Dartmoor the shortest distance between two points is seldom a straight line.) Dartmoor bogs and mires are numerous but seldom dangerous. They can however be very inconvenient and wet feet early in the day can spoil a pleasant trip. Unless you are exploring a river valley, try to gain height steadily and, once gained, try to maintain it – the views are better from high ground and the going is often easier.

Observe the Country Code – shut all gates, keep dogs on leads and deposit no litter. "Take nothing but photographs and leave nothing but footprints."

Ramblers must understand that a large part of northern Dartmoor is used for live firing by the Ministry of Defence. There are three Range Danger Areas – Merrivale, Okehampton and Willsworthy and when a range is in use for live firing the area is closed to the public. The area of each range is denoted by a line of red and white posts and on firing days red flags (or in the case of night firing, red lamps) are flown from a number of high points just outside the boundaries of each range. It is dangerous to pass the line of red and white posts when such signals are being flown. Lists of firing dates and times for the ensuing week are displayed at Post Offices on and around the Moor and are published each Friday in the *Western Morning News*. Details of firing programmes can also be obtained by using the telephone answering line on 01803 559782.

It will be seen that the instructions for the detailed walks that follow assume that ramblers will arrive at their intended starting place by car. The fact is that if one has to rely on public transport a long walk is often necessary before the intended ramble can begin. Nevertheless it is possible to explore much of Dartmoor by using public transport and details of what is available can be obtained locally. Dartmoor has a good public transport network operating throughout the summer months, and other services are available at other times of the year. For general enquiries and other visitor information please telephone the National Park Authority's High Moorland Visitor Centre, Princetown on 01822 890414.

It does sometimes happen that people get into trouble on the Moor, through illness, exposure or accident. The Dartmoor Rescue Group exists to deal with these emergencies. They can be contacted at any time of the day, no matter what the weather, by telephone – dial 999 and tell the operator what you want.

Lastly, please read the relevant chapter thoroughly before you set out. Otherwise you will not know until it is too late that your chosen expedition lies within a firing area, or that it is not one that you ought to attempt in the prevailing weather conditions. Be prepared and you will enjoy your Dartmoor.

EXPLORATION 1. Scorriton, Chalk Ford, Mardle valley, Hapstead Ford, Sandy Way, Michelcombe.

(CLEAR OF ALL FIRING AREAS)

Starting place:
Scorriton, near Holne. Map reference 703685.

Approach:
From Exeter, Torquay, Newton Abbot, Bovey Tracey, etc. via A38 turning off at Buckfastleigh, leaving town by way of Chapel Street and taking route signposted Holne.
From Okehampton, Tavistock, Plymouth, etc. join A38 in vicinity of Plymouth then proceed as above.
From Moretonhampstead, Chagford, etc. either follow A382 and join A38 two miles beyond Bovey Tracey; or leave Moretonhampstead by B3212 turning left in four miles at the Watching Place, then follow signs towards Manaton to Heatree Cross, go straight on towards Haytor by way of Swallerton Gate and Harefoot Cross, fork right at Hemsworthy Gate to Ashburton, then join A38 (turn right towards Plymouth) turning off at Buckfastleigh, and proceed as above.

Amenities:
All amenities at Ashburton and Buckfastleigh. Public house (Church House Inn) at Holne. Public house (Tradesman's Arms) at Scorriton.

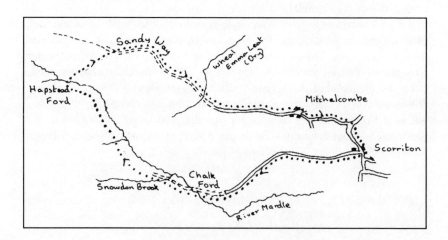

Parking for the exploration: *There should be no difficulty about parking at Scorriton, but do please remember that this is a community where people have to go about their daily lives. Park considerately and do not cause an obstruction.*

Buzzard

Type of excursion:
Not an arduous walk, mixed countryside with a good many tracks and paths. A few short steep climbs. Some open moorland. About 6 miles.

We start this walk at Scorriton, a tiny village, not even possessing a parish church. In fact it lies in West Buckfastleigh but to most people it possesses an affinity with Holne rather than with its mother town. We leave the village by the green road – unfit for motor vehicles – which runs west and south-west along the ridge between the Holy Brook and the River Mardle. This lane runs for a little over a mile between fields and at the further end begins to lose height and then comes down to the Mardle at Chalk Ford. Just before our track begins to slope down to the ford another track goes off through a gate on the right across Scorriton Down. This is not now regarded as being a public right of way, though the opposite used to be the case. On reaching the ford we find that we can cross the stream in comfort by means of a fine footbridge. This was installed by the National Park Authority, to replace the old one, a clapper, which disappeared many years ago. In his *Guide to Dartmoor,* William Crossing refers to the bridge but gives no details. However, if we hunt about a bit we shall find the spot where the old bridge used to be and the stones from which it was formed lying in the stream. One of the stones bears the date 1815 and the initials I.G.

Having crossed the stream we take stock of our surroundings. We find we are at the bottom of a very steep valley, down which the Mardle flows from the NW. Behind us to the north and NE lies the rising ground of Scorriton Down with enclosures coming down to the water's edge. Ahead of us to the west, NW and south are the slopes of Buckfastleigh Moor, so steep as to cut off our view of anything more than a few yards distant. From the ford a track runs up the hill to the west for about a hundred yards when it is joined by three other tracks coming in from the NW, SE and south. Our track continues westward and upward for a short distance then veers north-westerly and soon reaches a little stream – the Snowdon Brook – which it crosses at a rocky ford. A little further on we meet another track coming in on our right. This has come up from the Mardle by a different route having started at the cross-ways that we left a little earlier.

We now continue along the track which traverses the steep hillside with the river a hundred yards or so below us flowing from the NW to SE. En route we pass through the ruined walls of a prehistoric enclosure containing a hut circle – this is Mardle Ring. At a point about a mile from Chalk Ford the track brings us down to the water's edge at a spot where there is a ford where in normal conditions it is possible to cross the stream. We do not do so however but continue upstream with the river on our right for another quarter-mile or so when we come to another ford. This is Hapstead Ford, an important crossing in times gone by for here wayfarers making their way across the moor to places as diverse as Princetown, Hexworthy, Dartmeet, Widecombe and elsewhere would converge upon the ford to make the crossing. The name Hapstead is also borne by an ancient estate on the outskirts of Buckfastleigh, about four miles away.

Foxglove

At Hapstead Ford we cross the Mardle and on the further side we find a track leading away from the ford in a north-easterly direction. At first it is a fairly steep climb but soon becomes less so; then, keeping a careful eye on the compass we find that the track is veering away to the SE. It is now time for us to leave the track and take to the open moorland, pursuing a course almost exactly NE for about a quarter of a mile. Soon we strike a very well marked track running more or less east and west across the open moor. This is Sandy Way, an ancient track and much used in the early 19th century by farmers and tradespeople who lived in the vicinity of Holne and Ashburton.

At this period the prison at Princetown was occupied by French and American prisoners of war. A weekly market was held at the prison and to it went the country people to trade with the prisoners. The latter used to make a variety of toys and ornaments from wood and bone and these they used to barter for provisions and other small luxuries brought by the country folk. Eden Phillpotts' famous novel *The American Prisoner* contains some vivid descriptions of this market. Sandy Way commences at Michelcombe, for which we are now bound and traverses the moor to the edge of Fox Tor Mire near Whiteworks. It there connects with another track which brings the wayfarer safely to Princetown. From Michelcombe to Princetown as the crow flies is about $7^1/_2$ miles – to the walker it would be more like ten.

Having reached Sandy Way we turn right and walk along it for nearly a mile until we reach the edge of the enclosures where there is a gate in the wall. About 200 yards before we reach the wall we shall see that the track is intersected by a shallow gully running more or less north and south. This is the dry bed of the Wheal Emma Leat which we shall meet again when exploring the valley of the Wo Brook – see Exploration No. 3. From this point the leat flowed along the contours of the down and rather less than a mile further on fell into the Mardle to do its work at the copper mines further down stream. On reaching the gate – the place is called Lane Head – we pass through noting as we do so that yet another track diverges here. This one goes off to the SW and if followed would bring us back to the Mardle again, about three-quarters of a mile below Hapstead Ford.

From Lane Head we follow the steep and rocky lane for rather less than a mile. At the bottom of the lane we pass through a gateway at a spot where another track goes off to the north making for Holne Moor. On the further side of the gate we find the public road, which literally ends here, and just beyond and to the left the hamlet of Michelcombe. This is but a tiny cluster of farms and houses and there is little to detain us. The map shows it as being the site of a blowing house (a tinners' smelting house) but personally I have never been able to identify it. We pass through the village and soon reach a fork in the road. We take the right hand branch. A quarter of a mile on we come to another junction and again bear right down a steepish hill to reach our cars at Scorriton.

EXPLORATION 2. High Down, Brat Tor, Bleak House, Rattlebrook Head, Great Links Tor, Lyd valley.

(PARTLY WITHIN THE OKEHAMPTON FIRING AREA)

Starting place:
High Down near the Dartmoor Inn, Lydford. On A386 Okehampton to Tavistock road, three-quarters of a mile ENE of Lydford village. Map reference 522853.

Approach:
From all directions via A386 by way of Okehampton or Tavistock.

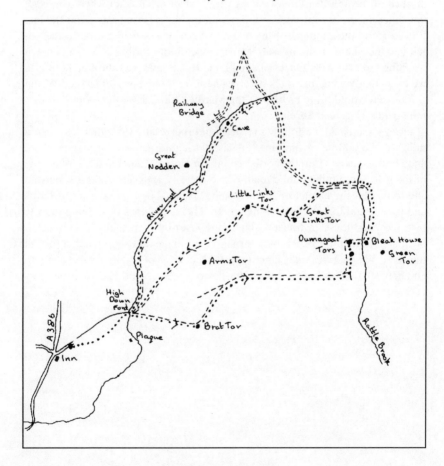

Amenities:
Public house (Dartmoor Inn) at starting place. Public house (The Castle), Post Office, shop and toilets at Lydford. All amenities at Tavistock and Okehampton.

Parking for the exploration:
At the top of the lane, as described below.

Type of excursion:
This is wild open moorland country with some paths and tracks. Some steepish climbs but nothing too exhausting. **This is not an excursion to be attempted in any but a spell of settled weather unless an experienced guide is available.** *About 9 miles the round trip.*

Red Grouse

The focal point for explorers essaying this trip is the Dartmoor Inn. This stands on the east side of the A386 road rather less than a mile east of Lydford but the true starting place is on High Down behind the inn. To reach the down we drive up the narrow rough lane which leaves the main road just north of the inn, passing through a gate which should be shut unless it is obviously left open on purpose, and bear right to the car park.

We start off by following the line of the track which runs NE across the common. At this stage we have the wall of an enclosure on our left and open country on the right. Ahead of us we see Brat Tor with its distinctive cross and to the north of Brat Tor, Arms Tor. We are going gently downhill and after about half a mile we reach the banks of a stream – the River Lyd, from which Lydford takes its name. The track reaches the river at High Down Ford. (Wheal Mary Emma Ford is a little further downstream.) Here we cross the river; there are a footbridge and stepping stones as well as the ford. Before doing so however, if time permits, we can walk south along the bank above the stream for a couple of hundred yards or so until we reach Black Rock. This is a miniature tor which overlooks the river and here there is a seat and a plaque attached to the rock in memory of Captain Nigel Ratcliffe Hunter who was killed in the First World War. The inscription on the plaque reads as follows:

> In loving memory of Captain Nigel Duncan
> Ratcliffe Hunter, MC and Bar, Royal Engineers,
> who was killed in action at Biefvillers, near
> Bapaume, on March 25th 1918, aged 23 years.
> He loved the Moors of Devon and on his last visit
> to Lydford he wrote the following lines:
> Are we not like this moorland stream
> Springing none knows where from,
> Tinkling, bubbling, flashing a gleam
> Back at the sun; e're long
> Gloomy and dull, under a cloud;
> Then rushing onward again.
> Dashing at rocks with anger loud,
> Roaring and foaming in vain.
> Wandering thus for many a mile,
> Twisting and turning away for a while;
> Then of a sudden 'tis over the fall,
> And the dark still pool is the end of all.
> Is it? I thought as I turned away,
> And I turned again to the silent moor.
> Is it? I said, and my heart said "Nay",
> As I gazed at the cross on Widgery Tor.

Widgery Tor is the name often given by local people to Brat Tor, which we are about to visit.

From Black Rock we return to the ford and cross the river. On the further side we shall find a track running away from the stream and going NE and rising steadily to cross the col between Brat Tor to the south and Arms Tor to the north. We shall also find a much narrower path running SE and mounting the fairly steep side of Brat Tor. We take the latter path and after a steady climb of nearly half a mile – with frequent stops to admire the view – we reach the summit of the tor and the cross which surmounts it. This is Widgery Cross and it differs from all other Dartmoor crosses in that it is constructed from dressed blocks of granite instead of being the more normal one-piece type. It was erected at the cost of Mr. W. Widgery, a well known local artist, to commemorate the Golden Jubilee of Queen Victoria in 1887. It fits in very well with the local scenery and is a landmark for miles around.

Widgery Cross

As is to be expected from so elevated a spot, the views from Brat Tor are very fine and allow some tempting glimpses into the fastnesses of the Forest. We now turn away from the tor and make our way down the boulder encumbered hillside in a north-easterly direction. At a distance of about a quarter of a mile from the summit of Brat Tor we strike the old mine track which has come up from the ford below by way of the steep slopes of Arms Tor which now lies to the north of us.

We turn right along the mine track and follow it up the moderate slope of the hillside, noticing as we go the many excavations near the track, the work of the old tin miners. About half a mile from the point at which we first struck this track it begins to veer to the SE and a little further on it forks, the right hand branch going even more decidedly SE, the other to the NE. We follow the latter, which soon turns almost due north and begins to run along the contour

Great Links Tor

of the land. We now have below us to the east the fairly deep valley of the Rattlebrook and above us to the north and west the high ground, about 50 feet higher than our own elevation at the moment, upon which stands those two strangely named tors, Higher and Lower Dunnagoat. If we decide to visit these tors we shall assuredly need to stop to regain our breath in the course of the climb.

This will give us a chance to conjecture about the origin of the name they jointly bear. As is usual with Dartmoor place names there is nothing definite about this. Crossing suggests that the name may be derived from the Celtic *dun,* a hill, and *coed,* a wood, or trees. He adds that there are still a few trees to be found in the valley below. On the other hand the authors of *The Place Names of Devon* say, quite positively, that Dunna Goat is referred to in a document dated 1588 as Dunyng Gate and add: "The 'gate' must have been one of the forest boundary marks". Was it? Certainly the forest boundary runs nearby, along the course of the Rattlebrook in fact, but where Dunyng Gate was, if it ever existed, I cannot say.

The northernmost of the two tors is Higher Dunnagoat and to this we make our way, drinking in as we go the dramatic scenery now presented to us. Right opposite the tor, on the further side of the valley of the Rattlebrook, will be seen a ruined cottage and about 300 yards east of that is Green Tor. Like those we have just visited this is not a very spectacular tor, but it may be thought worth a visit because of its isolated and desolate position and its

Bleak House

considerable altitude – it stands at 1762 feet above sea level. Be that as it may, the cottage is a must, almost as much a Mecca as is Cranmere Pool to the Dartmoor explorer.

This lonely place is known as Bleak House, and never did a dwelling bear a more appropriate name. The building is now ruinous but formerly it seems that it was the home of the resident representative of the West of England Compressed Peat Company. Bleak House features in Eden Phillpotts' novel *The Whirlwind*, but the author calls it Dunnagoat Cottage. To get to Bleak House we have to cross the Rattlebrook – no difficulty about this – and now we continue on the same side of the stream, walking northward. As we proceed we notice that man has been at work again.

Intermittently, over a period of just about a hundred years, tens of thousands of tons of peat have been removed from this part of Dartmoor. The first records are dated 1868 and ten years later the company just mentioned was established here with the intention of processing peat for fuel. They built a factory and constructed a tramway for the conveyance of men and peat to and fro between the village of Bridestowe, where it connected with the main railway line, and the workings. The industry never flourished however and half a dozen companies were formed and each in turn failed before the whole thing closed down in 1955. The result of this attempted exploitation of Dartmoor's resources has been to lower the level of the ground in quite a dramatic fashion over an area of several acres in the vicinity of Rattlebrook Head. This, the source of the stream, lies about 600 yards north of Bleak House and to it we now make our way.

Sleeper bridge –
Rattlebrook Head

Even the most fervent lover of the Moor cannot claim great beauty for this particular spot, the grim signs of man's activities being too plain to see. Apart from the morasses caused by the removal of the peat there are piles of broken bricks and shattered masonry, piles and coils and sheets of rusty metal with mud and stagnant water everywhere. All this results from the demolition of the abandoned buildings which once housed the processing machinery. Surely, if you are going to knock 'em down you should tidy them up as well? Still, we have had a splendid and interesting walk to get here and now we see, within a National Park, the kind of mess which helps to make conservationists so importunate.

Having examined the ruined peatworks we now turn to the west and here find the track of the former tramway, plain to see and to follow. There are no tramlines of course. We follow it along and find that it rises for a couple of hundred yards, then levels out for a short distance before it begins to fall. Soon the track begins to veer away, first towards the NW then almost due north. When we are at a distance of about a quarter of a mile from the peatworks we see that we have to our left and about 400 yards away the rocks of Great Links Tor. This is truly one of Dartmoor's great tors and if we have time in hand this is a good opportunity to visit it. This can be done by making our way to it direct, taking such advantage of the contours as we can.

Having explored the tor and admired the views we can if we wish shorten our journey (at the expense of some rather rough going) by taking a course across the common to Little Links Tor, which bears almost NW from its bigger brother. A little over a half a mile due west of Little Links Tor lies the valley of the Lyd. On reaching this all we need to do is to turn left (south) downstream and this will bring us in about a mile to High Down Ford, where we crossed the river earlier in the day.

Assuming that we do not wish to shorten the walk, on leaving Great Links Tor (or if we do not visit it) we continue along the line of the tramway until it brings us to a crossways. Here we meet the River Lyd, flowing towards us from the right and just emerging from the bog in which it rises. Here we leave the tramway and follow the river instead. This takes us through an area that has been much disturbed by the tinners; indeed this is true of the river valley for the next mile or so. Close by the spot where we leave the tramway and not far from the river bank is a tiny cave, nature assisted by the hand of man no doubt, which is reputed to be a tinners' shelter and also to have been used by smugglers "long ago".

As we continue downstream along the Lyd we find that the ground to the west of the river is rising and becoming more and more precipitous. We are in fact passing beneath the very steep slopes of one of Dartmoor's strangest hills.

This is Great Nodden, which seen at a distance and from some angles has the decided appearance of a pudding turned out of its basin and inverted. This hill is composed, not of granite but a kind of shale which, in loose particles, covers pretty well the whole of its surface. The division between the granite and the metamorphic rock actually runs down the river valley. As we proceed we find that the ground is greatly encumbered with loose boulders which make careful negotiation a necessity.

These conditions have of course been brought about by the activities of the old tinners of whom traces can still be seen all the way down the valley.

At a point about two miles from the spot where we first joined the river we pass below Arms Tor towering above us to the east and then, having crossed a little brook, we meet the track coming up from High Down Ford and making for the saddle between Arms Tor and Brat Tor. In a few yards the track brings us to the ford itself and here we re-cross the river and make our way up the rising ground to our cars near the Dartmoor Inn.

EXPLORATION 3. Holne Moor, Horn's Cross, Wo Brook, Hexworthy mines, Down Ridge, Skir Hill, Horse Ford, Saddle Bridge.

(CLEAR OF ALL FIRING AREAS)

Starting place:
Combestone Tor, near Hexworthy. Map reference 670718.

Approach:
From Plymouth, Tavistock and Okehampton, to Two Bridges then via B3357 to Hexworthy Cross 4$^1/_2$ miles east of Two Bridges, there turning right and passing over Huccaby Bridge and through Hexworthy.
From Chagford and Moretonhampstead by way of B3212 to Two Bridges, left on to B3357 then right at Hexworthy Cross as above.
From Exeter, Torquay, Bovey Tracey, etc. via A38 to Ashburton, turning off at Peartree Cross (watch for Two Bridges signs) then to Hexworthy Cross (half a mile beyond Dartmeet) there turning left for Huccaby Bridge and Hexworthy as above. **Be ready for narrow steep and winding roads beyond Hexworthy Cross.**

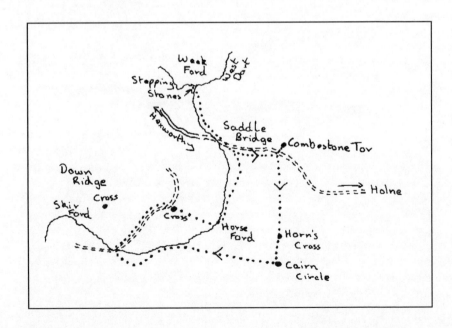

Amenities:
Public house (Forest Inn) at Hexworthy. Toilets, cafe, etc. at Dartmeet. Public house (Tavistock Inn) and Post Office and shop at Poundsgate (on B3357 2½ miles east of Dartmeet).

Parking for the exploration:
Large free car park at Combestone Tor.

Type of excursion:
Pleasant moorland walking, mostly easy going with a few steep climbs of no great length. About 4 miles.

Fallen rock basin – Cumston Tor

This expedition begins at Combestone Tor (which is always called Cumson or Cumston Tor by local people). The tor is very close to the road and consists of several rather low piles of rocks. As a tor therefore it is not very impressive. But if before starting our exploration proper we walk just a few yards to the north, beyond the tor that is, we shall begin to get glimpses of the splendid scenery for which the valley of the Dart is famous. So beautiful is it in fact and so easy of access that we might even be seduced away from the walk we originally intended. For your guide however this must not be, so we now turn away from the river valley and investigate the moorland instead.

On leaving the car park at the foot of the tor we cross the road and make for the highest ground to the south. We are here on Holne Moor, the common land pertaining to the parish of Holne and now happily in public ownership in the shape of the Devon County Council. Our path becomes well marked as we pursue our southerly course up the gently rising ground and we see ahead of us an object which soon proclaims itself to be an ancient granite cross.

This is Horn's Cross and it marks the route of the old monks' path which connected Buckfast Abbey with Buckland and Tavistock in medieval times. We shall meet this old track several times in our explorations of southern and central Dartmoor. In this vicinity we shall find several long, apparently endless, low banks of earth and stones and also a number of prehistoric hut-circles.

Horn's Cross

The long low banks are called reaves and there is a very large complex of them in this part of the Moor. Very little was known about them until the 1970s and 80s when investigation of them and other adjacent remains seems to have shown that the reaves are almost certainly prehistoric boundaries. They are probably not as old as the oldest hut-circles but are perhaps contemporary with the more recent huts.

The spot at which Horn's Cross stands used to be known as Stascombe's Telling Place. Staddiscombe is a farm near Holne and it seems that the farmer habitually mustered his sheep at this spot to count them.

From the cross we turn to the west, leaving the old monks' path for the time being, and make our way along the contours for half a mile or so. (Before doing this we can if we wish make a short diversion of about 300 yards or so to the SSW where are some more prehistoric remains in the shape of a cairn and a circle of stones surrounding a burial. These are easy to find when the bracken has died down, not so easy in high summer when the bracken is up.) About half a mile from Horn's Cross we shall find that we are descending into the valley of the Wo Brook and one of its little tributaries which comes in from the north. Wo Brook itself pursues a very winding course around Skir Hill, and in its vicinity are very many signs of the activities of the ancient tin-miners.

At one time, probably in the 18th century, there were two mines working here, the strangely named Henroost Mine and Hooten Wheals. Later they were combined as the Hexworthy Mines and continued work until well into the twentieth century. A thorough examination of these remains would take a very long time, but among other things that can be found, besides ruined buildings,

*Remains of dressing floors,
Hooten Wheals, Hexworthy*

are wheel pits, buddles (for washing the ore), dressing floors and blocked adits and shafts. In the valley on the SW side of the stream will be found a track connecting the ruins of Henroost with the those of Hooten Wheals.

If we follow this track we shall come to a clapper bridge spanning the brook. The bridge is clearly comparatively modern, having been constructed in the 19th century for the purposes of the mines. But it is interesting to notice how little it differs from other bridges of the same kind but several centuries older – obviously new ideas did not permeate very rapidly in remote districts like Dartmoor.

We cross the bridge and follow the track it serves up the gentle slope to the NE. At the top of the rise and to the left of the track we find the ruins of some buildings. So badly knocked about are they that it is not easy to establish their original purpose. However it is known that these were dwellings, occupied by workers at the mines in the 19th and early 20th centuries. Unfortunately the houses were used for target practice by troops training on the Moor during the war, otherwise we might have a better idea of the conditions in which tinners and their families lived some hundred years ago.

The track we are following is now running NE/SW and we continue along it for another three hundred yards or so. Then we see to the right and just clear of the track another ancient stone cross. This also marks the ancient track we left at Horn's Cross and now we leave the track we have been following and turn off right, down a gully formed along the line of the side track. This hillside is very steep here and a certain amount of care is needed in descending it.

Soon however we arrive at the stream at a point   *Horse*
where there is a crossing place called Horse Ford.   *Ford*
                                                       Cross
This used to be a proper ford but a few years ago
the stream rose in spate and washed out the ford, piling
the rocks from the river bed in a higgledy-piggledy pile.
It is still possible to cross however and this we do,
reminding ourselves as we do so that we are now
leaving the Forest of Dartmoor and re-entering the
parish of Holne, the stream – the Wo Brook – being
the boundary.

Our route now lies along the line of the stream to the north, but before we
leave the vicinity of the ford a little further exploration will be rewarded. It
will be noticed that in addition to the track along the stream that we are to
follow another track also leaves the ford at this spot and strikes uphill to the
SSE. This again is the monks' path and if we follow it for just a few yards we
shall find first an artificial channel carrying a full head of water – the Holne
Moor leat – which puts water into the Venford reservoir about two miles to the
east and then a dry channel, over which the track is carried by a little clapper
bridge.

This latter channel is the Wheal Emma leat, which has an interesting history.
It seems that in the mid-19th century there was something of a minor boom in
mining in the vicinity. In particular two copper mines in the valley of the River
Mardle near Buckfastleigh were combined and worked as one. But the amount
of water in the Mardle was insufficient to work the mine machinery and,
lacking a better supply, a leat was engineered to bring water from the
Swincombe river on the edge of Fox Tor Mire. The route followed brought the
leat to the north of Ter Hill and Down Ridge. It crossed the Wo Brook in an
aqueduct near Horse Ford and then continued along the contours of Holne
Moor finally to empty its water into the Mardle about 3 miles above
Buckfastleigh. The leat has long been disused and the aqueduct over the Wo
Brook is no longer to be seen, but the dry channel can still be followed for the
greater part of its length and provides a useful guide and footpath for explorers like ourselves.

We now turn to the north and follow the line of the Wo Brook. The going is
mostly good with a few rough or splashy patches. We are walking along the
bottom of a deep valley and soon, looking away to the NE we see traffic
moving along the road near which stands Combestone Tor where we left our
transport earlier.

The track we are on is, as indicated earlier, a branch of the monks' path and
in earlier days was used by people who had come from the direction of

Saddle Bridge

Buckland or Buckfast and who were making for Dartmeet or Widecombe or places in that direction. At a distance of about half a mile from the ford we emerge upon the road, which crosses the stream by means of a bridge – Saddle Bridge. This is a charming spot, combining the beauties of ancient bridge, rocky river scenery and open and in places almost precipitous moorland. Close by the bridge, on the eastern side, will be found a ruined rectangular building. This formerly housed a Pelton wheel, an early form of turbine, which generated electricity for the tin-mines we examined earlier.

To regain our car all that is now necessary is for us to follow the line of the road up the steep hill to the east. Combestone Tor is on top of the hill about 600 yards away. The best plan is to keep to the common on the south side of the road and some distance from it. Although steep, the going is not bad and frequent rests are justified to take in the glorious scenery. Also there are two splendid hut-circles rather less than half-way up which demand examination.

If on arrival at Saddle Bridge we feel that we have a little time in hand a minor diversion along the footpath which continues alongside the Wo Brook* beyond the bridge will be well rewarded. The brook falls into the West Dart below Week Ford which is about 600 yards north of Saddle Bridge. The river scenery both along the brook and in the vicinity of Week Ford (where there is a splendid set of stepping stones) is spectacularly beautiful and no words of mine could possibly do justice to it.

* Have you been wondering all this time why the map calls it O Brook and I call it Wo Brook? Or have you been puzzled by the very odd name – there is little to choose between O Brook and Wo Brook is there? As to which is right you takes your choice; some authorities call it one thing, some the other. It has had various names through the centuries – Ocbrooke, Okebrook and Wobrooke among them from 1244 onwards. What does it mean? The authorities are uncertain but think it might be derived from "oak brook", though as they say, oaks are rare here. They were probably less rare before the tinners cut them down and made charcoal from them to smelt their metal!

EXPLORATION 4. Merrivale, Longash, Hucken Tor, Davytown, Whithill, Ingra Tor, Yes Tor Farm, Swell Tor Quarry, King Tor, Longash Common.

(CLEAR OF ALL FIRING AREAS)

Starting place:
Car park south of road 300 yards east of Merrivale Bridge.
Map reference 552750.

Approach:
From Tavistock by way of B3357.
From Plymouth via Yelverton and Princetown by B3212 then on to B3357.
From Torquay and Newton Abbot via Bovey Tracey, Manaton, following signs towards Moretonhampstead, then Princetown and Tavistock.
From Exeter, Chagford and Moretonhampstead by way of B3212 to Two Bridges then on to B3357.

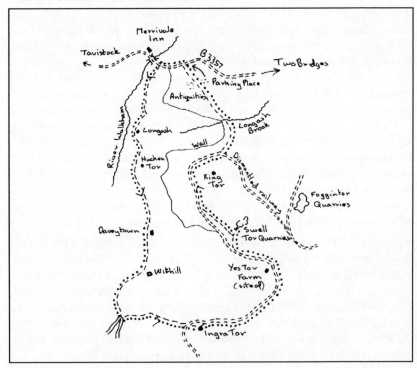

Amenities:
All amenities at Tavistock and Princetown. Public house (Dartmoor Inn) at Merrivale.

Parking for the exploration:
Ample off-road parking space (free) at starting place.

Type of excursion:
This ramble includes about 2 miles of bridle paths, a long section along the disused Princetown railway (positively no trains!) and also some open moorland. Good going all the way with only one moderate climb. About 7 miles.

Staddles, or rickstands, at the deserted site of Hucken Tor Farm.

Having parked we return to the road and turning left walk along the road towards Merrivale Bridge. Just before reaching the bridge however we see a sign on the left indicating a bridle path. We turn into this and pass through the farmyard of Hillside and into the lane beyond. This runs between fields with the River Walkham in the valley below us on the right for about a third of a mile. We now reach another ancient farm, Longash. This no longer functions as a farm, however, the fields having been sold off. We pass behind the farmhouse, which was being renovated when I last saw it, and into the lane which continues beyond. About 200 yards beyond the house we enter a small wooded area and here reach a little bridge spanning a stream – the Longash Brook – which we shall meet again towards the end of our excursion. This is a beautiful little stream which comes tumbling down the hillside in its rocky bed to meet the Walkham in the valley below.

If we hunt about a bit in the vicinity of the bridge we shall find the site and remains of the former bridge, probably a clapper, which was superseded many years ago. The path now leaves the wood and runs through the enclosed land, though the walls on our left are now so low and ruinous as almost to have ceased to exist. These were formerly the fields of a farm named Hucken Tor Farm and if we leave the track and walk into the grassy area on our left we shall soon find the substantial ruins of Hucken Tor farmstead.

Here we see what was once the farmhouse, a longhouse in which the human inhabitants lived at one end and the animals at the other and also other buildings: stables, barns, outhouses and the like. There is also a rectangular area with a number of stone pillars about two feet high standing erect upon it. These stones are staddles and upon them the rick of corn – oats, rye or barley – would be built so as to keep the crop clear of the ground and hopefully beyond the reach of rats and mice. How long it is since Hucken Tor Farm was occupied is doubtful, almost certainly not in living memory. We are told however that there is a record of the farm and its tenant as far back as 1317, when it was part of the lands belonging to Buckland Abbey.

We now return to the track and follow it south as before. Soon we enter another wooded area where the trees are almost wholly smallish oaks growing among the rocks which in ages past have fallen from the tor which stands just clear of the track. The tor is Hucken Tor, sometimes called Okel Tor, and from it the ancient farm we have just visited took its name. A little further along the track we come to a gate. As we pass through we notice that the gate is hung upon the rocks of the tor. It is suggested that the first farmer here used the tor as his southern boundary and hung his gate – probably a pole – upon a hook driven into the tor; and from this the name of the tor and the farm derived.

It is so beautiful a spot that time spent here cannot be wasted. Eventually however we move on, continuing southward as before. At first the track runs over open common but soon we have enclosures on both sides and now we come to a farm – Davytown – on our left and then a lane on our right which leads to another farm, Parktown. The track has now developed into a good hard road and soon enters a wood and crosses a tiny stream – the Yestor Brook – at another beautiful and enticing spot. Just beyond the wood we reach Whithill, another farm.

Wood Sorrel

*Crane bases –
Ingra Tor*

Here the road bears away to the right and comes round in a loop to a crossroads about a quarter of a mile south of Whithill. We now turn left and follow the road which rises fairly steeply for a quarter of a mile until it comes to a cattle grid on the edge of the common and here it stops. Beyond the cattle grid a track goes alongside a wall towards Criptor, but we take a side track which goes off to the right towards Routrundle, and where it bends to the right we leave it and carry on ESE across the rising ground. This will bring us in about a quarter of a mile to the foot of a group of rocks called Ingra Tor and also to the line of the abandoned Princetown railway. In the days when this branch line was working there was a halt at Ingra Tor, established it is said, for the benefit of ramblers.

This is also said to have been one of the few railway stations in England which displayed a notice warning passengers of the danger of snakes.* It is true that there are adders to be found on Dartmoor, but in my experience they are seldom seen. There are also perfectly harmless grass snakes, but whatever kind you may come across the best plan is to leave them severely alone – they are just as frightened of you as you may be of them and very anxious to get away from you.

Having reached the dismantled railway track near Ingra Tor we now turn left and walk along the track as it winds its serpentine way towards Princetown. At this stage the line is running NE/SW across open moorland and from this vantage point the views are stupendous, especially to the west, north-west and north. Below us to the west lies the wooded valley of the Walkham and above

*This warning notice can still be seen in the small railway museum at Saltram House, near Plympton, which is owned by the National Trust.

and beyond this as it bends round from the north is a tremendous backcloth of tors – Great Mis and Little Mis, Great Staple and Middle Staple, Roos Tor and Cox Tor, Vixen Tor and Feather Tor, Heckwood Tor and Pew Tor – all are in view as the eye sweeps the circuit. On a sunny day with good visibility this is one of the noblest sights in Devon and perhaps in England.

As we walk towards Princetown we have marshy ground below us to the west and on the further side of the marshy area, about a quarter of a mile away, the little farmstead of Criptor, whose farmlands come right up to the edge of the railway track. Soon the track begins to bend round to the west and passes over the valley of a little stream – the Yestor Brook again. Here the careful observer will notice enclosure walls on the eastern side of the track which seems to enclose a loop-shaped corridor which leaves the track we are follow-ing, crosses over the stream and returns to and crosses the track we are on. This is the abandoned route of the original tramway along which horse-drawn trains used to run before the days of steam. This section of the old line had to be abandoned when the new line was engineered because of the tightness of the bends.

Just beyond the Yestor Brook we notice the substantial ruins of two or three buildings a little to the west of the track. This was the site of Yestor Farm, which ceased to be inhabited many years ago. The fields of this farm seem to have been incorporated with those of Criptor Farm lower down. Our track is now running along a sort of shelf on the steep hillside which gradually becomes very rocky. We now reach a spot where at some time there has obvi-ously been a gate across the line. If we here leave the track and climb the high bank to the NE we shall find that a few yards will bring us to the spoil heaps and ruined buildings of the old Swell Tor granite quarry. This quarry, which ceased to work in the 1920s, operated in conjunction with Foggin Tor quarry, less than half a mile away to the NE.

There is much here to explore, including the huge quarry in the hillside below Swell Tor itself. This quarry, with Swell Tor and King Tor, lies within one of the great loops in the disused railway we have been following. This line first opened in 1823, with horse-drawn trains, and closed in 1956. The line never really paid its way but one of its prime functions was to transport the stone from the quarries nearby. Swell Tor quarry was connected with the railway by means of an inclined plane running more or less NW from the quarry buildings.

If having examined the buildings and other remains we now walk NW along this inclined plane for a couple of hundred yards or so, we shall see a number – about a dozen in fact – of large worked stones lying to the right of the track. These are about 8 feet long and 3 feet high and resemble huge brackets made to support a shelf. It is said that these stones – corbels is their proper name – were made about 1903 as part of a contract to supply stone for the widening of London Bridge. The corbels were intended to support the weight of the additional footways built out over the river, and those still here were surplus to requirements. It is also said that some of the surplus corbels from Swell Tor were shipped along with the material from the bridge when it was demolished and exported to Arizona in 1971.

Following the line of the inclined plane we regain the track of the old railway just south of King Tor. The rocks of this tor are of no great height but standing on a promontory above Longash Common it provides some very striking views of the valley of the Walkham and the tors to the north. We follow the old track round King Tor to a point where we have the tor immediately behind us to the south. Facing north we are looking out over Longash Common and immediately below us, about 400 yards away, is the valley of the Longash Brook.

Down into this valley we now make our way, making for a field wall ahead of us. On reaching the wall we do not enter the field but turn right and follow the wall around until we come to the edge of the brook. The ground here tends to be rather marshy and care is necessary if wet feet are to be avoided. On reaching the brook we search about for a convenient place to cross and having done so climb the high bank on the other side, noticing as we do so the tinners' gullies and similar works in the vicinity.

We are now in the immediate vicinity of the Merrivale antiquities. To the west and close to the wall which runs westward from the brook will be found the Longstone, a pillar of granite about 11 feet high. Nearby are some other shorter stones and a little to the north a circle of standing stones about 62 feet

Stone rows – Merrivale

in diameter. It seems certain that the Longstone was once the terminal stone of a stone-row which has largely disappeared – probably to build the wall nearby. These remains and the other monuments that we shall visit are all attributed to the Bronze Age. It is clear that these monuments were of great ritual significance to the builders, but their actual purpose is unknown.

About 200 yards north of the Longstone we shall come to the two double stone-rows for which Merrivale is famous. One is 180 yards long, the other nearly twice that length. The latter (southern) row is very unusual in that the row is broken midway by a burial place consisting of a ring of stones and the remains of a kistvaen. Just to the south of the southern row traces of a shorter row at an angle to it can be seen.

Nearby also is a splendid kistvaen, one of the largest on Dartmoor. This is complete with cover-stone which has had a section cut out of its middle, presumably because someone needed a gatepost or something similar.

The two long stone-rows are separated by a leat and the ground in the vicinity tends to be marshy. This can be avoided by going round the western end of the rows and then striking in a north-easterly direction. We are now quite close to the road and less than half a mile from our car. Before returning to it however we should take the opportunity to examine the hut circles and enclosures associated with them south of the road. These also are of Bronze Age origin, but not so the huge circular disc of granite which lies among them.

It is said that a well known 19th century antiquary mistook this for the cover-stone of a kistvaen, unique because it had obviously been shaped by man. We know better however; it was shaped in the early years of the 19th century and was intended to be the edge-runner of an apple crusher used in cider making, but for some reason was abandoned before completion.

It may be too that in the vicinity of Longash Common we have noticed one or more erect pillars of granite with "T" engraved on one side and "A" on the

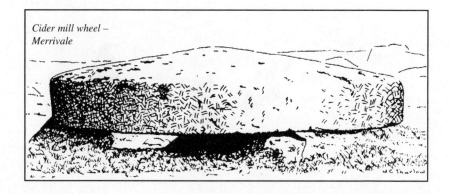

Cider mill wheel – Merrivale

other. These are waymarks, dating from the late 17th century and mark the ancient trackway across the moor from Tavistock to Ashburton. We are now only about two or three hundred yards from the car park, the best route to which lies along the grassy path on the left of the road.

N.B. A full and interesting account of the Merrivale antiquities can be found in Chapter 8 of *Prehistoric Dartmoor* (Forest Publishing) by Paul Pettit.

EXPLORATION 5. Manaton, Hayne Down, Swine Down, Jay's Grave, Natsworthy Gate, Mariners' Way, Easdon.

(CLEAR OF ALL FIRING AREAS)

Starting place:
Manaton Church. Map reference 749812.

Approach:
From Torquay, Newton Abbot, Exeter, Totnes, etc. via Bovey Tracey.
From Tavistock, Plymouth, etc. via Two Bridges then B3212. Turn right after about 10 miles at The Watching Place crossroads.
From Okehampton via Moretonhampstead turning right on to B3212 and left at The Watching Place crossroads after 4 miles.

Amenities:
All amenities at Moretonhampstead, Post Office/shop and public house (Kestor Inn) at Manaton. Public house (Warren House Inn) on B3212 2 miles NE of Postbridge. Toilets, Post Office/shop and public house (East Dart Hotel) at Postbridge.

Parking for the exploration:
Large car park adjoining churchyard at Manaton.

Type of excursion:
Easy moorland walking, much of it along tracks, some of which will be muddy during a wet period. Only one steep climb of no great length. About 6 miles.

Since we are starting this excursion next door to the church it would be a pity not to visit that beautiful old building, but it is suggested that the visit be deferred until the end of the trip – we will come back through the churchyard!

Having parked, we leave the car park by the southern entrance and find that we are almost at a crossroads with the village green to the left. At the further end of the green will be seen a long low white house. This was formerly the village inn, the Half Moon, but is now a private residence. Grouped around the green are a number of other ancient cottages, some of them thatched, and opposite us is the building which was for many years the village school and adjoining it the school house. This grouping around the green presents a very pleasant picture and there are those who feel that Manaton has lost something

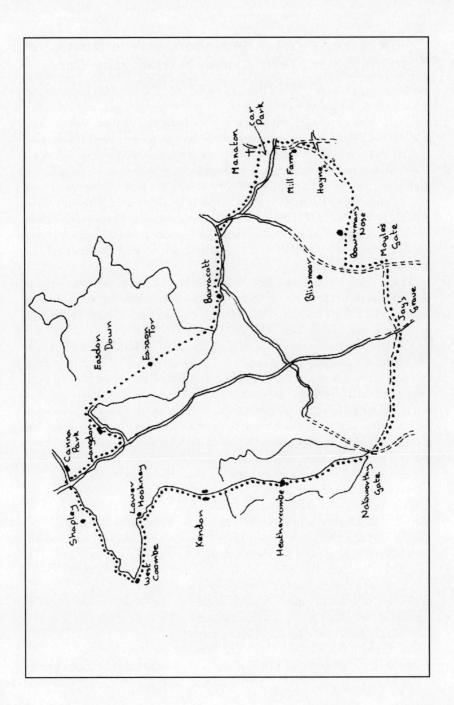

39

worth having, now that the inn is half a mile away on the Bovey Tracey road and the children of the village have to go to school elsewhere.

Having taken in our surroundings we now move off. First we walk along the lane which runs southward from the crossroads. Passing Mill Farm we see a footpath sign by a gate on the right. We go through the gate and cross the field diagonally to the left. At the far side we leave the field and emerge into a rough lane. Here we turn right and follow the lane up the steep hillside, past a farm and along the winding lane up hill until we emerge upon the open common beyond, where there are tracks which go to the top of the hill. We follow the most distinct path, which goes to the right above a stone wall, and we see ahead of us the rocks of what can only be called a tor. The summit of this hill, whose name is Hayne Down, is a more or less level plateau which is greatly encumbered with rocks of many sizes. At either end of the plateau are concentrations of huge rocks which are sometimes referred to collectively as Hayne Down Tors.

At the north-western end, just below the highest point, will be found a feature famous in Dartmoor scenery and folklore. This is Bowerman's Nose, a natural rock pillar consisting of layers of rock piled one upon the other and standing about 25 feet high. The topmost layer is so shaped as to give the impression of a human figure wearing a peaked cap. In former times this was identified as a rock idol and of course the Druids were held to be responsible. We now know that this strange figure is the result of natural weathering over many thousands, perhaps millions, of years. The name Bowerman has also exercised the imagination of many people in the past. There is an old account which states that a person named Bowerman lived nearby in William the Conqueror's day, the suggestion being that the rock took its name from him – but is it perhaps the case that he took his name from the rock …? Who knows, the derivation of Dartmoor place names is a notoriously imprecise study.

Having examined Bowerman's Nose and enjoyed the splendid scenery all around we now leave the hill top and make our way down the steep incline to the west. This brings us in about 400 yards to the moorland road below, on the further side of which lies a cottage name Blissmoor. On reaching the road we turn left and walk along it for about a third of a mile to a spot where there is a gate across the road. This is Moyle's Gate and here we turn to the right without going through the gate and walk up the gently sloping hillside, alongside the wall. Our path breasts the hill and continues down the other side where it reaches another road at a spot where there are a few trees and a gate across a lane which starts on the further side of the road.

On reaching the road we notice that between ourselves and the gate just mentioned, on the road-side verge, is a grassy mound reminiscent of a grave;

Bowerman's Nose

an impression which will be heightened if, as is very likely, there are flowers or greenery adorning the mound. Here is another famous Dartmoor spot, for we have found Jay's Grave. Kitty Jay is said to have been a late 18th or early 19th century parish apprentice who, having been abandoned by her lover when she found herself pregnant, hanged herself in a barn not far away. Because she had taken her own life this poor child could not be buried in the churchyard and was instead interred here where two moorland tracks converge upon the Chagford/Ashburton road. There is a tradition that fresh flowers or greenery will always be found upon Jay's Grave and that no-one knows who puts them there. But I know – you put them there, and so do I and other sentimental people like us. It is only a very few years ago that I was told by an acquaintance who had recently come to live near Jay's Grave that a few days after their arrival she was told by one of their very few neighbours that she ought not delay in "paying her respects to Jay". That, it transpired, meant that she should place some flowers on the grave or she "would never prosper". Thus is folklore made. John Galsworthy's short story *The Apple Orchard* is said to be based upon the story of Kitty Jay. As Galsworthy lived at Manaton for many years this seems not unlikely.

From Jay's Grave our path lies through the gate and along the rather muddy lane – a bridle path – beyond. This pursues a course which is somewhat north

Jay's Grave

of west for about three-quarters of a mile. At first we have trees to our right and a wall bordering fields to the left, but after a while the trees cease and after that we have enclosures on either side. At the end of the lane we emerge upon a narrow road; this is the Natsworthy Valley road which connects Widecombe to the south with Long Lane to the north, this in turn connects with the B3212 Moretonhampstead/Two Bridges road. We turn left into this road and notice as we do so that on either side of the road are granite gateposts, now without the gate which used to span the road. This spot is Natsworthy Gate and nearby is the ancient Natsworthy Manor House. Having walked just a few yards to the south we now see a gate on our right with a footpath sign alongside. We go through the gate which gives access to the open moor at the foot of Hameldown, more often called Hameldon. There is a pretty little stream here, the East Webburn River, which comes dashing down the hillside on its way to Widecombe and beyond. Our path however, which is clearly marked, does not ascend the hill, but veers to the right and enters a wood which it traverses from south to north for a mile or a little more.

The path we are following is quite famous. It is called the Mariners' Way and it is said that in medieval times it crossed Devon from north to south and that along it used to come seafarers who, having been paid off at a north coast port, Bideford for example, were now making their way to a port on the south coast – Dartmouth perhaps – in search of a new berth. It is also said that rest houses were established along the track for the benefit of wayfarers. We shall visit one of these reputed rest houses a little later on, but alas the authenticity of this pleasant legend cannot be guaranteed. Most of this ancient track is now lost, but part of it, to the north of where we are now, in the vicinity of Chagford, forms part of the Two Moors Way. This is a long-distance footpath which spans Devon from Ivybridge in the south to Lynmouth in the north, a distance of 103 miles.

About half way through the wood we emerge into a clearing which is really the fields belonging to a farm, Heathercombe. We approach the farmhouse across a field and passing close to the house emerge upon a road which runs to right and left. On the other side of the road is a cottage and on the left of this a gate through which we go and again enter a wood. Our track is now running almost due north but a little way along it forks. Here we must be careful to take the left hand track which will soon bring us to the end of the wood across the northern end of which runs a rough lane. Opposite us is a gate giving access to a field across which the track goes to the farm of Kendon. Beyond Kendon the track crosses more fields, first in a northerly direction but later veering to the NW. A little over a quarter of a mile beyond Kendon we enter another rough lane which we follow to Hookney, a collection of farms of which Higher and Lower Hookney are two. At Hookney, where a tarmac road comes in from the right, our track turns left (almost due west), and in a short distance we go through a gate on the right. Our route crosses several fields until it emerges above Coombe, another collection of houses and farms of which the principal is West Coombe.

Here will be found the building reputed to have been a rest house or hostel for travellers in days gone by. We approach the house by way of a ladder stile and a little bridge, and go through the open doorway ahead into a short passage, emerging through another doorway on the other side. The inference is obvious – the traveller arrived at night and entered the hostel to spend the night. In the morning he left by the other door and proceeded on his way – voilà!

At West Coombe, at the side of the road, will be found a small round stone building with a conical roof, also of granite. The roof is covered with turf and the building is equipped with a door and a window aperture which is also fitted with a small door. This is an ash-house, a feature frequently found near these old moorland farms. In times past when the main domestic fuel was peat and

Hard fern

"Slot-and-L"
gateposts – Manaton

houses contained much timber and thatch in their construction it was the practice to remove the embers of the fire before the family retired for the night
and place them in the ash-house. This removed the danger of fire from the
house and also preserved the valuable ashes in a dry condition so that they
could then be used as manure on the thin acid Dartmoor soil. Waste not –
want not. The ash-house at West Coombe is one of the best specimens still to
be found in the vicinity.

From Coombe the Mariners' Way continues to the NW along what must be
one of the muddiest lanes in Devon. However, it is now time for us to leave
this old track and instead we take the lane which runs northward then veers
away to the east and NE, by-passing the farm of Shapley and bringing us out
into Long Lane at Canna Park. We now turn right into Long Lane and follow
it for about half a mile until we reach another lane coming in on the left. Here
we turn left and after a short steep climb reach the two farms of Higher and
Lower Langdon. We come to a T-junction, from where Lower Langdon lies
downhill to the left, but we turn right and climb up a narrow rocky track. At a
point about 300 yards from the farms we find a side path on our right; following this, we reach a gate on the other side of which is the open hillside of
Easdon Down (East Down). The rocky summit of the down is now about 300
feet above us and if we want to avoid the steep climb all we need do is contour
the hillside to the south and east. On the other hand the climb need not be too
abrupt if we take the easiest route which lies to the north and east and the
views from the summit are so spectacular that the effort is well worth while.
Just to the south of the summit rocks, a little below the highest point, will be
found the great rock named Whooping Rock on the map. There are two
versions of how this rock got its name. One is that its configuration is such that
a whooping noise is produced when the wind sets in a particular direction. The
other is that on this hilltop mothers used to expose their children who were

suffering from whooping cough so that they might be in the vicinity of the sheep which were grazing on the down. Whooping cough was a killer disease in those days and several odd cures and customs must have come down to us in consequence.

From the summit of Easdon we make our way down by the easiest route which lies to the south. This brings us after about a quarter of a mile to a sunken lane which skirts the foot of the hill on the south and west. We enter and follow this lane and soon reach a farm named Barracott (on the left) and a cottage called Bowermans (on the right). Just past the cottage we again emerge into Long Lane and turn left. A quarter of a mile further on we see a stile on our right and a footpath sign close by. Crossing the two fields on the other side of the stile we emerge through a gate into Long Lane and continue SE for a further quarter of a mile when we enter another footpath on the left. This brings us directly into Manaton churchyard by the western gate.

Just inside this gate is the churchyard cross. This is a tall pillar of granite which has been roughly shaped into the form of a cross. It stands in a carefully shaped socket stone which clearly does not belong to it. It is said that in the 1840s a new rector came to take charge of Manaton Parish. He was very displeased to discover that his parishioners had a curious rite through which they went whenever someone had died in the parish. This consisted of carrying the coffin three times round the churchyard cross before the burial took place. The rector tried to persuade his people to discontinue this survival from a pagan age, but failed to do so and instead took the law into his own hands. One night the cross disappeared; everyone was sure that the rector was responsible but he never admitted it and it was never found.

However, early in the 20th century the present cross was found supporting a wall nearby. It is said to have been brought to the churchyard in the belief that it was the missing specimen but although this was clearly not the case it was nevertheless adopted and has remained in situ ever since. The original is still missing. Leaving the cross we walk through the churchyard and find *Cross* ourselves upon the village green, close to where we *at* left our transport earlier in the day. *Manaton*

EXPLORATION 6. Avon Valley and Dam, Zeal Plains, Eastern and Western White Barrows, Petre's Pits, Bala Brook.
(CLEAR OF ALL FIRING RANGES)

Starting place:
Shipley Bridge, South Brent. Map reference 681628.

Approach:
From all directions by way of A38 and South Brent, leaving the village by road signposted Avon Dam.

Amenities:
All amenities at South Brent. Toilets at Shipley Bridge (spring to autumn only).

Parking for the exploration:
Large free car park at Shipley Bridge.

Type of excursion:
Some paths and tracks but mostly open moorland walking, tussocky and splashy in places but nowhere unreasonably so. This is a very "up and down" walk but fortunately the "downs" fully compensate for the "ups". About 8¹/₂ miles the round trip. This can be considerably shortened if desired.

Shipley Bridge, the starting place for this expedition, lies in one of the most beautiful areas in the Dartmoor borderland. The bridge itself, probably an 18th century construction on the site of a much older crossing place, spans the Avon river some miles from its source in the desolate heart of southern Dartmoor. The river for about two miles above the bridge is spectacularly beautiful, especially in times of spate, as we shall soon discover.

Before setting out upon our walk there are some matters of interest in the immediate vicinity of the bridge that are worth noting. Adjoining the car park several large stone buttresses each with a long slot-like aperture in it will be seen. On the other side of the road from the car park there are obvious signs of former buildings and a variety of bumps and hollows in the greensward. All these remains are relics of long vanished industries. For a period in the 19th century this was the site of a naphtha distillery, where this highly volatile and inflammable oil was distilled from peat brought down in huge quantities from the moor. When this enterprise failed the buildings were taken over by a

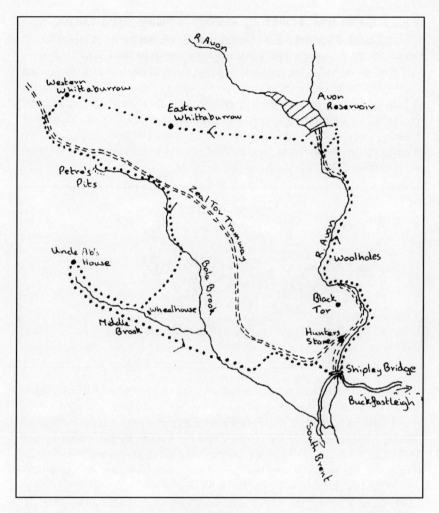

company involved in mining and refining china clay, also obtained from the moor. On the high ground above the car park will be found the granite lined filter beds and settling pits also associated with the china clay industry and we shall have a look at them later on. After some few years this concern also went out of business because, it is said, of the low quality of its products. Ramblers interested in bygone industries will find these remains well worth exploring.

A good hard road, open to pedestrians but not to wheeled traffic, runs from Shipley Bridge to the foot of the Avon Dam nearly two miles away and along this our route now lies. This is a favourite promenade for local people and holiday-makers who do not feel inclined for more arduous or ambitious walking. For us however it is but an opening stroll, but very beautiful and full of interest. At a point about a quarter of a mile from the bridge we shall see a side road going off to the left; this leads to the water filtration works on the high ground nearly half a mile away. By the side of the road at the intersection of the two roads a squarish block of granite about 30 inches high will be seen. This will be found to bear a variety of inscriptions consisting of a number of names – Treby, Carew and Trelawney among them. The stone is known as the Hunters' Stone and the names are those of prominent members of the foxhunting fraternity of Victorian and Edwardian times.

The Hunters' Stone

Just beyond the Hunters' Stone the river falls over a beautiful little waterfall and just beyond this the road passes through a gateway. The gate will be found to be padlocked but there is access for foot passengers at the side and on passing through we enter the grounds of what used to be Brentmoor House. This was a small mansion which later became a Youth Hostel and then fell into ruin when the property was bought by the water authority. It was finally demolished as an exercise by the Royal Marines.

We are now passing through an area thick with rhododendrons on either side – a fine sight when they are in bloom. On the left, raised upon a rock among the bushes, will be seen a small memorial with an inscription in memory of the little daughter of a Mr. Meynell who once lived here. Shortly we pass the site of Brentmoor House where little more than the foundations are to be seen and very quickly emerge into open country. We now see that we are walking up a long deep valley with steeply sloping sides. We still have the river on our right and the rocks of Black Tor high above us on the left. Soon we come to a bend in the river and here the road passes over a bridge and we now have the river on our left, coming towards us from the north down the valley which locally is called Long-a-Traw, meaning the long trough, which it greatly resembles. We now notice that the ground on our right has flattened out somewhat; this flat area is called Woolholes Plain – Woolholes being the clitters of rock associated with it.

There is nothing here to indicate the reason for so strange a name but it seems likely that wolves lived hereabouts in former times and that the name is a survival from those days. The wolf is said to have been exterminated in England in the Middle Ages but it may have survived longer in remote places, especially in the vicinity of a Royal Forest such as Dartmoor.

The Avon Dam

A few hundred yards further on and ahead of us we shall see something resembling a great wall blocking the valley to the north. This is our first glimpse of the dam at the foot of the Avon reservoir. This was constructed in the mid-1950s and provides water for much of South Devon. As we draw nearer we see that the road we are on veers to the left and crosses the river again before coming to an end at the foot of the dam. For the time being however we do not want to cross the river but instead take a rough track which leaves the road and, rising with the land, makes for the right hand end of the dam. On arrival at the dam we shall find that it stretches away to our left (SW) for nearly 400 yards and that the level of the water is well below the point at which we have arrived.

The post and wire fence which formerly enclosed the reservoir has been removed. The area can be dangerous however; the banks are very steep and the water deep. Children in particular should not be allowed near the water's edge.

Standing at the end of the reservoir and looking north we see in front of us the Heights of Hickaton Hill and beyond that Puper's Hill on Buckfastleigh Moor. To the NW lies Huntingdon Warren with the site of the old warren house in full view. In front of it lies the valley of the Western Wella Brook, flowing down to fall into the Avon near Huntingdon Cross.

We now leave our elevated position and make our way back to the road by the nearest practicable route. This will bring us to the end of the bridge near the foot of the dam. We cross the river and make our way almost to the end of the road close to the dam. Here we find a path on the left which mounts the steep grassy bank and brings us after a short stiff climb to the end of the dam on the western side. Here we can rest and admire the view and the great sheet of water lying below us.

Having rested we turn our faces to the west and begin to climb. Our course should be almost due west with just a touch of north. The ground rises steeply for the first three or four hundred yards and then more steadily for another half a mile or so. Eventually we reach the summit and now find that we have in full view an object that appeared on the skyline some little while ago. This is a great heap of stones with a strange round turret on top which gives it something of the appearance of a submarine.

Eastern Whitaburrow

This is Eastern Whitebarrow – Eastern Whittaburrow in local parlance. It is possibly a prehistoric burial place; perhaps the remains of some Bronze Age chieftain lie beneath the stones. It is about 250 feet in circumference and about 30 feet high. It must contain some thousands of tons of granite boulders; one wonders how the primitive folk who raised it managed to find the time and energy as well as supplying their own bodily needs. Personally, I do not think that the round turret is part of the prehistoric structure. My guess is that this was superimposed upon the cairn when the latter was adopted as a boundary mark, in medieval times or later.

It may be that we shall decide to eat our picnic lunch in the shadow of Eastern Whittaburrow; there is very little other shelter nearby. Then we turn again to the west, or rather to the WNW and make our way along the crest of the ridge. At first we find a path which we welcome as it conducts us across the very broken ground with a minimum of difficulty. But the path soon disappears and we find the going rather rough as we negotiate the ancient tinners' works and peat ties with which the top of the ridge is strewn. Soon however we see our next objective ahead of us. This is another cairn, Western Whittaburrow this time, which stands nearly at the north-western end of the ridge at a distance of about three-quarters of a mile from its eastern counterpart.

As we approach this great heap of stones certain differences become apparent. For example there is no turret on top of this one and the stones of which it is composed are much more scattered than in the last. Also, as we draw nearer we see what seems to be a stone post sticking up from among the stones. On reaching the cairn the reasons for the difference in outline become apparent. On the summit of the scattered pile we find the unquestionable remains of a rectangular building. The stone post is just that, but it has the respectable name of Petre's Cross, as you shall hear.

At some time in the first half of the 19th century the nearby peat ties were being worked for the benefit of the naphtha distillery at Shipley Bridge. The workmen lived on the job and built themselves a house on Western Whittaburrow from the stones of the cairn. They reached a stage in their building when they needed a long stone to act as the lintel above the fireplace (you can still discern the fireplace in the ruined building). Nearby they found an ancient stone cross, Petre's Cross, which had been erected in the 16th century to mark the boundary of the Manor of Brent. The workmen uprooted the cross and having knocked off its arms built it into the fabric of the building above the fireplace. Many years later, the naphtha industry having failed, the house became ruinous and eventually it was more or less demolished. Among the ruins was found the mutilated cross which was then again erected to fulfil its old function of a boundary stone, but this time it was planted upside down. the broken tenon which fitted into the missing socket stone can still be seen at the top of the shaft.

Our principle source of information about this place is William Crossing's *Guide to Dartmoor*. He also tells us something about the diet of the workmen who built the house on the cairn. It seems that they largely lived on rabbits which they poached from Huntingdon Warren, less than a mile away across the river to the north.

From the cairn we turn to the south-west and in about a hundred yards reach a shallow trench, about 6 feet wide, which runs NW/SE down the hill. This is the bed of a former tramway – the Zeal Tor tramway – which served the nearby peat ties. We turn SE and walk along the tramway, from which the wooden rails were removed many years ago. Here and there however the granite sleepers can still be seen with the iron spike which secured the rails in position. For one very short length is it still possible to find the remains of one or two of the actual rails.

At a distance of about three-quarters of a mile from the cairn there is a mile stone inscribed "Shipley – 2 miles". This used to stand by the side of the tramway but now has fallen into the trench. A $^3/_4$-mile stone stands a little further to the SE. We have now reached a spot where there is a wide shallow valley to the right of the tramway. This is Petre's Pits, from which the china clay was dug to be sent down to Shipley Bridge. On the further side of this valley large quantities of tinners' spoil can be seen, showing that they also dug and delved in this vicinity.

Zeal Tor Tramway

A little stream rises in Petre's Pits. This is the Bala Brook, whose name probably means "the mine brook". The stream pursues a winding course and eventually falls into the Avon a quarter of a mile or so below Shipley Bridge. As we follow the stream along we shall see that it is well named, for the old tinners have been very active here, and there is scarcely a yard of the stream that seems not to have been interfered with. At a distance of about half a mile below Petre's Pits we shall find that the course of the brook is now descending very rapidly and that at the same time the high ground on our right is falling back from the stream.

We now cross the stream and strike away from it to the SW, following the contours as far as possible. This will bring us, in a little over a quarter of a mile, to the valley of the Middle Brook, a tributary of the Bala Brook. Our aim is to strike the Middle Brook about halfway along its course, close to the spot

Wheelhouse – Middle Brook

where there is a ruined building on the north bank. This building was clearly connected with tin-mining in some way and judging from its construction probably housed a set of stamps for crushing the tin-ore. A couple of hundred yards further upstream is another structure which almost certainly housed a water-wheel, also connected with the tinners.

On the high ground on the south side of the valley, almost opposite the last described building and only about 50 yards from the stream will be found a more or less circular enclosure, another hut group of the Bronze Age folk. Incorporated in the wall of the enclosure, at the point closest to the stream will be found a tiny building only about six feet long, the roof of which has partly fallen in. I doubt very much if this is part of the original Bronze Age complex and tend to think that it has some much more recent origin, perhaps in connection with the tinners who have been so very active in this valley.

We now continue our exploration of the valley upstream. We find that the stream is getting progressively narrower and the ground more and more encumbered with the waste produced by the tinners in their search for metal. To the north of the stream but running parallel with it only a few yards distant will be found a deep, narrow and rocky gully along which, it is quite clear, the tinners diverted the stream so that it might do their work of excavation for them, afterwards allowing it to return to its own channel. In one place the stream disappears altogether beneath the masses of tinners' waste, only to emerge again a little further on. This valley provides an extraordinary example of how hard these old tinners must have worked and emphasises the massive effect that man's activities can have upon a landscape.

The Middle Brook rises in a fold in the land called Petre's Pits Bottom and just beyond the source of the brook, at the head of the valley we find the ruins of another building. It is said that the horses used in connection with the old peat works used to be stabled here. The building is known locally as Uncle Ab's House. Probably Uncle Ab was the horse-keeper and lived on the job. Just beyond the ruin, lying on the greensward, will be found a slab of granite about 2 feet long by 18 inches wide. This bears the initials C.B. and the date 1809. No parish boundary seems to run nearby and the significance of the inscription is unknown to me.

We now turn and retrace our steps down the Middle Brook. If we walk along the southern bank we shall find the semblance of a path well above the stream which will take us past the enclosure we examined a short time ago and bring us, in rather less than a quarter of a mile, to another and somewhat different enclosure. This is shaped rather like a square except that one side of the square, that nearest the stream, is missing. This seems to be another example of later interference with a prehistoric compound and here again we find one of the

Uncle Ab's House

little buildings thought to have been constructed by the tinners to provide a safe hiding place for their valuables. Close to the rear wall of the compound will be found what at first glance appears to be a moss-covered pile of boulders. Closer examination reveals this to be a domed hut or cache, one of the best examples of a bee-hive hut I have yet found on Dartmoor.

We now leave the Middle Brook and strike away to the SE, along and down the steep hillside. This will bring us in about a quarter of a mile to the banks of the Bala Brook again. We should now take the first opportunity to cross the brook; in normal circumstances this will be achieved quite easily but in times of spate a more diligent search for a crossing place will probably have to be made. Once across the stream we turn right – that is downstream – and walk along the bank until we reach a post and wire fence. This encloses a water intake and here we turn left and follow the fence along uphill. At the upper corner of the enclosure we stop and take stock of the situation.

We are standing facing north about a quarter of the way up a steep hillside. Immediately to our left and just a few yards away is the tumbled wall of a Bronze Age enclosure. Adjacent to this, both within and without, are a few hut-circles. To our right and a few yards along the wire fence is another hut-circle and another ruined wall. The latter is part of a compound called the Half-circle, and that is just what it is. The wall forms a semi-circle based upon the stream and within it are a number of hut-circles. There is a similar compound on the further side of the stream also containing huts.

That this is an interesting place no-one can deny but the interest will be enhanced by a careful examination of the hut-circles close to the corner of the fenced-in enclosure. It will be found that in three instances tiny stone huts, with the remains of their domed roofs still visible, have been built in or in juxta-position to the prehistoric huts. These little huts are no more than four or five feet in diameter and one of them still has its doorway, complete with door-jambs and lintel, in position. The doorway is little more than two feet high. What have we found? Pixie houses? Tinners' caches? Dog kennels or pig-sties? I don't know, but as far as I am aware these little huts have never before been described in any book about Dartmoor.

From the corner of the fenced enclosure our route now lies nearly due east along the hillside. After about 300 yards or so we shall reach a wall with fields beyond. We now turn up the wall to the NE and after a short steep pull up we come to the end of the wall and there find the course of the old tramway which we left some time ago near Bala Brook. We turn right and follow the tramway along until it brings us to a made-up track. This is the drive which connects the Avon reservoir filtration plant with the road near Shipley Bridge. We cross the drive and continue across the open common in a south-easterly direction. We now see ahead of us a complex of great circular pits and rectangular filter beds.

These are the remains of the china clay works mentioned at the beginning of this expedition and they are associated with the ruined buildings close to where we parked our cars. It will be noticed that originally the circular settling pits were lined with granite blocks. These have largely disappeared over the years – after all granite blocks such as these are admirable building material, whether you want to build a house or a pig-sty!

A small chamber within a hut, Bala Brook

We are now very close to Shipley Bridge, which lies just below us to the east. At the southern end of the industrial site a steep, rocky (and sometimes muddy) track will be found. We follow this down to level ground and emerge upon the road close to the bridge and car park at the end of a fairly arduous but very satisfying walk of about 8$\frac{1}{2}$ miles.

EXPLORATION 7. Warren House Inn, King's Oven, Hurston Ridge and stone row, Heath Stone, Shapley, Hurston, Chagford Common, West Vitifer Mine.

(CLEAR OF ALL FIRING AREAS)

Starting place:
B3212 road just NE of Warren House Inn. Map reference 674809.

Approach:
From Torquay, Newton Abbot, etc. via Bovey Tracey and Manaton, following signs towards Moretonhampstead, then towards Princetown by way of B3212.
From Exeter via Moretonhampstead and B3212.
From Plymouth by way of Yelverton and Princetown on B3212.

Amenities:
Warren House Inn at starting place. Post Office/shop and public house (East Dart Hotel) and toilets at Postbridge.

Parking for the exploration:
Off-road parking near starting place, in various small car parks including Bennett's Cross $^1/_2$ mile NE of starting place.

Type of excursion:
Easy moorland walking, one or two steep short climbs but nothing to worry anyone in normal health. Some tracks and paths. About 7 miles the round trip.

The excursion starts quite close to the famous Warren House Inn, almost certainly the highest inn in Devon and claimed (though this is disputed) to be the highest in England. When I first knew it a peat fire was kept burning in the bar of the inn and was said never to have gone out in over a hundred years. It has gone now alas; practically no-one burns peat on Dartmoor these days.

The inn was the scene of a famous tale which must be told in a book such as this, familiar though it may be. The events described are said to have happened "long ago" which I take to mean probably the late 18th or early 19th century, before the inn was moved from the other side of the road. A wayfarer across Dartmoor found himself benighted and sought refuge at the inn. He was hospitably received and after supper was shown to a bedroom. On glancing round the room he noticed a large wooden chest and – his curiosity getting the

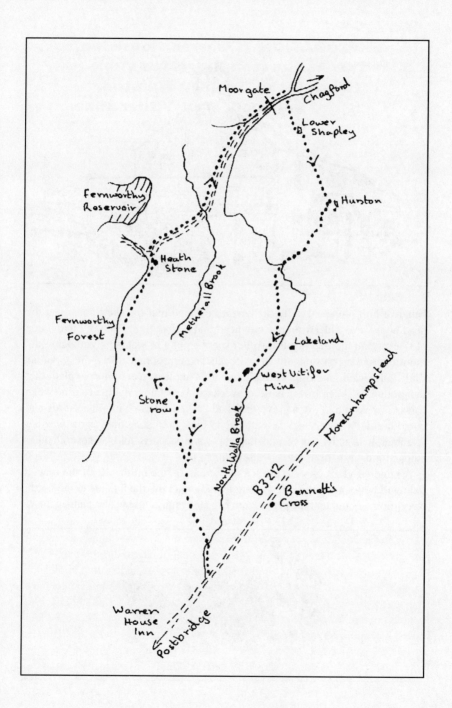

Warren House Inn

better of him – opened it. To his horror he found that the chest contained the dead body of an elderly man. Convinced that he had found his way into a den of thieves and murderers our traveller spent a night of waking dread but in the morning, finding himself still alive, he plucked up courage to enquire about his find. "Oh", said his hostess "that's father!" She then went on to explain that the ground had been frozen hard for weeks and her father dying at a time when it was impossible to dig a grave they had "salted him in"; in other words had cured him with salt as is done with bacon pigs, until such time as the weather relented. It is only fair to add that the same story is told of several other isolated inns in various parts of the country.

A hundred yards or so to the NE of the inn, on the north side of the road, a path will be found going off at an angle and mounting the hillside to the north. Very soon we find that the path is running alongside a low wall which encloses

Slotted stones – Bush Down

an irregularly-shaped area. The map shows, within this enclosure, something called King's Oven, which it describes as a ruin. In fact there is nothing here that can properly be described as a building though there was clearly one here in former days.

King's Oven is a famous name on Dartmoor. It was for long thought to have been a tin-smelting house in the early days of tin-mining. It is referred to in a document which is dated 1240 which describes the boundaries of the Forest of Dartmoor. In that document it is called *Furnum Regis*, which means King's Oven or Furnace. There has been a great deal of activity on the part of the tin-miners in the area spread over many centuries and this accounts for many of the great pits and gullies to be found in the vicinity. However, it has recently been shown that the name is more appropriate to the cairn on Water Hill, a short distance to the north-west.

Hurston Ridge

On leaving the enclosure which surrounds the site of King's Oven we continue along the path described for a couple of hundred yards or so but leave it when it begins to veer to the NNE and instead take a course that is almost due north. This will bring us to a higher point on the ridge and, at a point almost exactly a mile from our starting place, to the beginning of the Hurston Ridge stone row. This ancient monument, a relic of the people of the Middle Bronze Age, consists of a double row of standing stones, nearly 50 pairs in all. The row is 150 yards in length and has a badly robbed cairn (a burial place) at the south-western end and a transversely placed slab across the north-eastern end as though to close the row.

In 1900 the grave below the cairn was investigated by archaeologists and was found to contain a mass of charcoal and a broken pot, consisting of over a hundred fragments. It was not until 1960 that it was found possible to reassemble this pot when it turned out to be a vessel of clay 16 inches in diameter at the rim and 8 inches at the base. It had contained the cremated bones of the honoured dead. The vessel is thought to date back to 1300 – 1000 B.C. It is now in the Plymouth Museum.

From the stone row we take a north-westerly course, making directly for the edge of the Fernworthy plantations which are about a quarter of a mile away. By doing this we avoid a large marshy area around the head of the Metheral Brook which can be very unpleasant at times. On nearing the plantations we turn north along the edge of the wood and this will bring us in about half a mile to the road which comes up from Chagford and enters the plantations at this point, en route for Fernworthy reservoir. We do not enter the plantations however but instead take the line of the road to the NE.

Before leaving the vicinity, an examination of the greensward in the vicinity of the forest gate will be repaid. Here will be found a collection of little enclosures, surrounded by low stone walls. These are thought to be prehistoric fields, also of the Bronze Age. Among the stones forming the walls one much larger than the rest stands out.

This is the Heath Stone, a bound-stone of the Forest and also a waymark along the ancient track from Exeter to Tavistock which came this way via Chagford. Certain modern inscriptions will be found carved upon the Heath Stone. These were the work of a local man in the 1970s. He seemed to think that by defacing Dartmoor's ancient monuments he was serving the ends of the Christian religion.

The Heath Stone

On leaving the Heath Stone we follow the line of the road as described earlier. After about a mile we leave the open common by means of a gateway where there is a cattle-grid. A couple of hundred yards further on we reach the spot where another lane comes in from the left. On our right and opposite the end of the lane is a little stile on top of a high bank. We climb the stile and enter a field. We are now on the Mariners' Way, that ancient track which is said to date from medieval times and along which went the seafaring men making their way from the ports of North Devon to those in the south of the county or vice versa. We cross the field and emerge into a lane. This takes us to a farm – Lower Shapley – where we go through the farmyard (never mind the dogs; they are quite friendly). We now enter another field, skirting Higher Shapley farm, then across two more and out into a lane again. This in turn brings us to Hurston, Lower Hurston on the left, Higher Hurston on the right.

Higher Hurston is a splendidly restored and thatched longhouse, probably of 16th century date. We turn right here and go through a gate which takes us past the front of the house, then make for a gate over to the left. This gives access to a field which in turn gives on to a lane. We follow the lane for about 600 yards and then go through another gate beyond which is the open moor, Chagford Common again. We are now on a sloping hillside at the foot of which, on our left, runs a stream, the North Walla Brook. On the further side of the stream is the farm of Lakeland, surrounded by its little fields. Our course now lies almost due south and this will bring us to a ford which gives access to Lakeland (we do not cross however) and then to the site of the long abandoned West Vitifer tin-mine. During wet periods the ground in the vicinity tends to be marshy, but it can be traversed safely if care is exercised. In general it will be found that the hardest ground lies near the river bank.

The site and ruins of the West Vitifer tin-mine which we have now reached are interesting because among the ruins can be found the remains of three circular buddles or washing troughs. The buddle was a device for separating the sandy debris from the tin ore by washing, after the tin bearing rock had been crushed. It consisted of a circular trough in the centre of which was a boss upon which was mounted a revolving arm carrying either brushes of heather, etc. or flaps of sailcloth. The crushed ore was placed in the trough into which water was allowed to flow. The arm carrying the brushes, etc. then revolved, agitating the water. This resulted in the material in the trough being mixed with the water. The heavy tin-sand rapidly sank to the bottom but the lighter base material remained in suspension long enough to enable it to be run off with the water.

This operation was repeated as often as necessary to obtain a reasonable degree of purity when the remaining ore was removed for smelting. The force which worked the buddles was probably water power as the remains of two wheelpits can also be found on the site. However, it is known that elsewhere horse-power or even man-power was used for similar purposes. West Vitifer mine operated in the mid-19th century, from about 1850 to about 1870.*

On leaving the site of West Vitifer we turn to the west and find ourselves faced by a steep hillside. Up this hillside runs a gully, probably the remains of the original track which served the mine, and along this we make our way, following the track as it veers first to the north and then right round to the south-west. After a steep climb of about 300 yards the track comes out upon the flattened top of the ridge and merges with a path which runs almost due north and south. Here we turn south and follow the path which, after about a mile of easy walking, brings us back to the enclosure marked on the map as the site of King's Oven. Explorers with a taste for mystery and ingenious speculation may care to hunt about in the gully along which the path we are following comes down to the road. Here, if successful, they will find what may have been the course of a tramway used in connection with the tin-mining that went on hereabouts, and at the bottom of this two slabs of granite, each about 5 feet long, lying alongside one another but inclined at an angle from each other. On the upper surface of each of these stones will be found two smallish circular holes which are connected one with the other by slots cut in the granite. The exact purpose of these stones is unknown to me but I can only think that they were in some way involved in controlling the movements of the trucks along the tramway – if that is what it was. Over to you! We are now only a few yards from our vehicles and not much further from Warren House Inn and much needed refreshment – if we have timed our arrival cleverly!

* Readers interested in the mining remains on Dartmoor will find much valuable information in a booklet entitled *Dartmoor Mines* by Michael Atkinson, published by Exeter University in 1978.

EXPLORATION 8. The Staple Tors, Roos Tor, Cox Tor, the Windypost, Vixen Tor.

(CLEAR OF ALL FIRING AREAS)

Starting place:
Large free car park north of the road (B3357) half a mile west of Merrivale Bridge. Map reference 541750.

Approach:
From Tavistock by way of B3357.
From Plymouth via Yelverton and Princetown by B3212 then on to B3357 (turn left at Two Bridges).
From Torquay and Newton Abbot via Bovey Tracey and Manaton, following signs towards Moretonhampstead, then towards Princetown and Tavistock by way of B3212 and B3357.
From Exeter, Chagford and Moretonhampstead by way of B3212 then on to B3357 at Two Bridges.

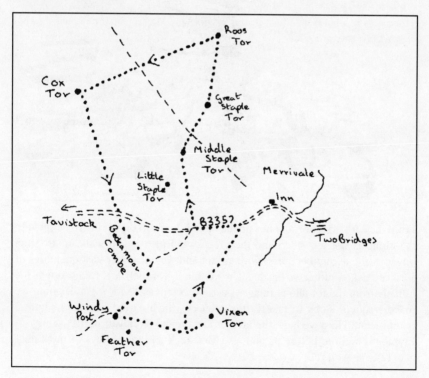

Amenities:
All amenities at Tavistock and Princetown. Public house (Dartmoor Inn) at Merrivale Bridge.

Parking for the exploration:
Car park at starting place.

Type of excursion:
Splendid moorland country – high moor and rocks and tors. One or two longish climbs but these can be taken care of by frequent stops to admire the magnificent views – anyway there is just as much down as up! About 6 miles the round trip.

Great Staple Tor

From the car park our route lies up the open hillside to the north. To begin with the climb is not too steep and the greensward pleasant to walk upon. Soon however the ascent becomes more abrupt and we encounter vast quantities of surface rock – clitter is the local word for it – which has rolled down the hillside from the tor above in ages past. To compensate for the stiff going we make frequent stops to take in the scenery which to the west and south is magnificent. Here we have the area of Devon and Cornwall in the vicinity of Plymouth laid out before us and also Tavistock and the valleys of the Tamar and Tavy as well.

There are matters other than scenery to be considered though and these are nearer to hand. An examination of the rocks among which we are making our way will reveal that many of them have been dealt with by man. In places it will be seen that a portion of a rock has been removed by drilling a row of holes in it. Wedges have then been inserted and driven home with a hammer with the result that the stone has split along the line of holes. Other rocks will be found that have been treated in this way but the operation never completed, with the result that the detached portion is still *in situ*. It is known that this method of splitting rocks was not introduced to Dartmoor until about 1800, evidence that the operations under consideration are comparatively modern. The fact is that a flourishing industry existed here in the 19th century. The workmen – sett-makers they were called – were engaged in making a variety of small artefacts from the surface granite (locally called moorstone), such as kerbstones, setts for paving and the like. Many towns up and down the country, of which Plymouth was one, were literally paved with Dartmoor granite.

A little further up the hill a number of low stone walls will be found, rather like small roofless buildings and, in or near them, numbers of small benchlike structures made from blocks of granite. The walls are the shelters erected by the sett-makers to protect themselves from the weather. The benches are sett-makers' bankers, i.e. the work benches at which the sett-makers stood to form the stone they were working on. It is said, with what truth I do not know, that when Castle Drogo at Drewsteignton was being built between about 1908 and 1928 the architect, Sir Edwin Lutyens, insisted on being supplied with weathered granite for the outer skin of the building and it was from this site that the stone was obtained.

Having spent some time in examining these relics of a now departed industry, we continue our journey up the hill. On more or less the same level as the site just described but a little further west stands Little Staple Tor and we can easily visit this if we wish to do so. But on this occasion we will defer such a visit and instead make our way up the hill to Middle Staple Tor which stands above us nearly half a mile from the road. This is quite an impressive pile of rocks but with no very special features so after a brief rest we continue upwards, still pursuing a course which is north with a touch of east. This brings us in another quarter of a mile to the rocks of Great Staple Tor.

This is one of Dartmoor's great tors and standing as it does at nearly 1500 feet above sea-level it provides a grandstand view of the countryside for miles around. The rocks of the tor too are spectacular. They are widely scattered but the central portion of the tor consists of two tall towers built up of layers of granite and so placed as to give the impression of a wide gateway. There are some good rock basins on the northern rocks. There is also a reputed logan stone (one which rocks if weight is applied to it) but I have never been able to identify it.

But most curious of all was the Staple Tor Tolmen – destroyed long ago. A tolmen is a stone with a hole in it and such stones were regarded as having magical properties – hence the witch-stones that hang in numbers by the doors of many cottages in Devon's sea-side villages. This was a tolmen with a difference however as it was made up of four stones. It stood on top of a rock with a flat surface, so providing the base. A smaller slab lay upon and to one side of the base and opposite this was a smaller roundish boulder, placed upon the very edge of the base. Superimposed upon the two latter was a slab nearly nine feet long by about six feet wide leaving a gap below through which an agile person might crawl. The old antiquaries attributed this to the Druids, a theory which is of course now exploded. But I for one am left wondering whether this remarkable tolmen was really a work of nature or if man did construct it how on earth he went about it.

From Great Staple Tor we continue northward for a further quarter of a mile or so. This is ideal Dartmoor walking; underfoot we have pleasant springy turf, slightly downhill at first then gently rising to Roos Tor (sometimes called Rolls Tor) which has been in full view ever since we reached Staple Tor. As we reach the summit we are presented with a splendid view over northern Dartmoor. To the north and east tor after tor present themselves to the view while immediately below us to the east flows the River Walkham in its winding valley with that doyen of all tors, Great Mis, on its lofty hill in a great loop of the river. To the west and south lie the farm lands of South-West Devon and East Cornwall with the sea beyond to the south.

Rock formation – Roos Tor

Once the impact of the stupendous views has subsided we can turn our attention to the tor. This again is not one of the most spectacular that Dartmoor has to offer, but it is very interesting, for a number of reasons. Upon the summit will be found two great masses of granite which from their appearance one would think at once were logans, i.e. rocking stones. In fact one of them, the northernmost, is marked upon the map as a logan but I have never been able to shift it. Also upon the tor are two or three fair sized rock basins, very nice specimens of their kind. These basins which also used to be attributed to the Druids are now known to be entirely natural, caused by the erosion of the softer or more brittle elements of the stone by the action of the weather over an almost infinite span of years.

Parted rocks –
Roos Tor

Beyond Roos Tor to the north extends a long ridge with a broad undulating top which merges into and eventually becomes that part of Peter Tavy Great Common known as Langstone Moor. To the NW and about a mile and a half away stands White Tor in the vicinity of which and extending down into the valley of the Walkham, to the east, are a large number of prehistoric remains of many different kinds. Among these is the menhir or standing stone from which Langstone Moor takes its name. There are also many hut circles, a badly robbed stone row and a once splendid stone circle which was shattered by artillery fire – the circle was used as a target by troops training during the Second World War. The view from the northern side of the rocks of Roos Tor is even more extensive than it was from Great Staple, especially to the north where many of the most distant parts of the Forest may be seen The observant explorer here will notice that Roos Tor is surrounded by a number of granite posts – I seem to remember 12 – each bearing a large incised letter "B". Alongside most of these posts are slabs or boulders of natural rock and each of these bears an incised circle, about ten inches in diameter, bisected by a straight line. It is on record that these posts and circles were installed in the 19th century on the instructions of the Duke of Bedford, the owner of the land, as a warning to quarrymen to come no closer to the tor in their search for workable granite. Here too it will be noticed that much of the surface rock has been attacked by the quarrymen, and the marks of their drills are everywhere.

We have now reached the turning point of our excursion. From the summit of Roos Tor our way lies almost due SW to the rocks of Cox Tor, just under a mile away. At first the land slopes gently downwards across the pleasant greensward. As we make our way towards Cox Tor we shall pass close to a considerable group of hut circles which we can visit if we wish. Running between the huts in this group in a direction more or less NW/SE is a well marked path which we are bound to cross en route to the tor. This path was formerly much used by workmen employed at the granite quarries at Merrivale and elsewhere. They used it to pass back and forth between their homes in the vicinity of Peter Tavy and the quarries. It is said that they used to mark the path by dropping shards of white pottery along it so that it could be seen even on the darkest night. A search along the path might well produce a few pieces of pottery in proof of the story.

Soon we reach the summit of Cox Tor, not too badly out of breath as this climb is less severe than is often the case. We now find that this is a very scattered tor indeed with the most massive rocks lying on the southern side below the summit of the hill. At the northern end of the hilltop are two or three large cairns, similar to many others to be found upon the Moor. These are perhaps the burial places of the Bronze Age folk who lived hereabouts. Cox Tor too provides us with magnificent views and on a warm sunny day this is a splendid place to linger and perhaps have our picnic.

Wheel wrights' stone
– Beckamoor Coombe

We leave Cox Tor by striking down the hillside on a course a shade east of south. This will bring us, in a trifle less than half a mile, to the Tavistock road which we cross near the spot where a long wide tinners' gully comes down the hill from the north and continues southward for some distance on the other side of the road. This great tinwork is formed along the line of a fold in the hillside called Beckamoor Combe and a little stream flows down the combe and also crosses the road. We follow the stream for about a quarter of a mile until we reach the spot where there is a boundary stone and here a path goes off to NE and SW. We veer SW and follow the path until it brings us to another stream, the Grimstone and Sortridge Leat.

This we should reach at a spot where an ancient stone cross stands beside the leat to mark the way. The cross is always called the Windypost these days, although its proper name seems to be Beckamoor Cross. It stands upon the Abbots' Way, the ancient track connecting Buckfast Abbey with Tavistock Abbey, on opposite sides of Dartmoor. How long this old cross has stood there no-one knows, but it is much more carefully shaped than is usual with these moorland crosses and may not be much older than 15th century.

Windy Post

The Windypost stands close to the foot of the rocks of Feather Tor, a low scattered pile which we can visit and explore if we wish. Our true course however lies due east across the common where about half a mile away we can see the high mass of Vixen Tor. We make for this, aiming at its southern side. On getting nearer we find that the tor lies within an enclosure: it is in fact on private land. The public is allowed access however, by means of a ladder-like stile over the wall and provided that no dogs are taken into the enclosure.

Vixen Tor is one of Dartmoor's most spectacular rock piles and will well repay a visit. Its situation, standing as it does on the slopes above the River Walkham, is beautiful in the extreme. The rocks are said to comprise the highest rock stack on Dartmoor and the shapes they assume from various angles are most intriguing. Seen from one angle the tor greatly resembles a couple on horseback with the lady riding pillion and embracing her groom from behind; from another viewpoint the Sphinx of Egypt is in evidence – there is no end to it!

Vixen Tor

If we have time in hand we shall undoubtedly want to linger in this delightful spot, but eventually we shall have to leave. We are only a little over half a mile from our cars. To reach them we leave by the stile and then turn right-handed around the perimeter wall which we follow round until we reach a path running NW/SW across the common. We now follow this path to the NE until it brings us out on to the Tavistock road just west of Merrivale. Here we turn left and find our cars a little further along the road to the west.

EXPLORATION 9. Fingle Bridge, Piddledown Common, Teign Valley, Dogmarsh Bridge, Fingle Gorge.

(CLEAR OF ALL FIRING AREAS)

Starting place:
Fingle Bridge, Drewsteignton/Moretonhampstead. Map reference 743899.

Approach:
From Okehampton by way of the A30 towards Exeter, taking the Moreton-hampstead road at Merrymeet Roundabout, through Whiddon Down, then turning left, and in a short distance left again to Drewsteignton; follow signs to Fingle Bridge.

From Exeter by way of A30 towards Okehampton, turning off at Woodleigh Junction, through Cheriton Bishop to Crockernwell, here turning left, and following signs to Drewsteignton and/or Fingle Bridge.

From other directions go first to Moretonhampstead, then take the A382 towards Whiddon Down and Okehampton, turning right at Sandy Park to Drewsteignton and Fingle Bridge.

Amenities:
Licensed restaurant (Angler's Rest) and toilets at Fingle Bridge. Public houses, Post Office/shop and toilets at Drewsteignton. Licensed hotel (Mill End) and Sandy Park Inn near Dogmarsh Bridge.

Parking for the exploration:
Car park beyond the bridge.

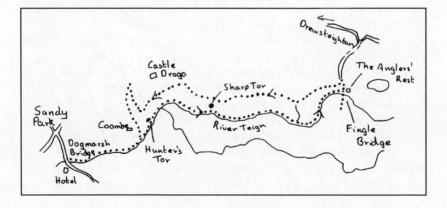

Type of excursion:

This is a walk which lies entirely along paths or tracks alongside the river and through the woods above the stream. The riverside path is rocky in places and there are one or two short steep climbs but nothing to worry people in ordinary good health. About 6 miles the round trip.

Fingle Bridge

Fingle Bridge stands at a spot famous for its beauty in a county full of beautiful places. The bridge (probably of 16th century date) is a packhorse bridge but wide enough to take a motor car. It is constructed entirely from granite, has three arches and is equipped with triangular bays in which pedestrians could take refuge when meeting packhorses with their projecting loads.

The hill above the bridge to the north is called Prestonbury and on its summit is a triple earthwork thought to be of Iron Age date. There is another similar one about three-quarters of a mile away to the south called Cranbrook Castle and a third named Wooston Castle a little further downstream, also to the south of the river.

It has been suggested that these were constructed as places of refuge to which the tribes could withdraw when danger threatened – perhaps at times when fresh arrivals from over the sea were known to be making their way up the valley in search of somewhere to settle. Certainly it would have been very difficult for an invader to have made headway against opposition if he approached from the west, south or east. From the north there is a much more moderate ascent.

We make our way upstream to the bridge, but before re-crossing we notice the very steep and rugged track which runs up the hillside almost from the foot of the bridge. This is a very ancient pack-horse track which zig-zags its way to the top of the gorge, passes close to Cranbrook Castle and finally emerges on to a road which connects Chagford with the Teign Valley and Exeter.

On the further (north) side of the bridge we do not take the riverside path opposite the Angler's Rest, but instead walk along the lane to the north and turn left into the path going to the west. This will take us along the river but at a much higher level, and will enable us to obtain magnificent views up and down the ravine. Our track converges with the Hunter's Path, and further on becomes part of the Two Moors Way. When we are nearly a mile from Fingle Bridge the path winds round the top of Sharp Tor, which we shall pass again on our return journey. For people with a good head for heights it is possible to stand on the summit of the tor and from this vantage point the most striking views are obtainable, especially up the valley towards Chagford where the town can be seen nestling beneath its protecting heights of Nattadon and Meldon Hill.

Beyond Sharp Tor the path we are following runs across Piddledown Common and for a time the woodland ceases. Now we begin to get glimpses of the open ground of Whiddon Park on the further side of the river. The adjacent Whiddon Park House was the ancient home of the Whiddon family. It was a daughter of this family who is said to have been shot dead at the altar by a jealous lover on her marriage day. The date of this occurrence seems to have been 1641; at least that is the date on Mary Whiddon's memorial in Chagford church. This incident is said to have been used by Blackmore in his novel *Lorna Doone* in which a similar happening occurs at Lorna's wedding to John Ridd.

A feature to look for in Whiddon Park is the very high stone wall which snakes down the precipitous hillside, separating the park from Whiddon Wood to the east. The purpose of the wall was to confine the deer to the park and so avoid the trouble caused by their wandering abroad.

Soon our path runs through another small area of woodland and bends southward with the river, passing above Hunter's Tor. Above us now we have the great granite house called Castle Drogo and its grounds. This is not the place for a description of Castle Drogo; suffice it to say that this splendid residence was built in the early years of the present century by a wealthy merchant named Julius Drewe who had as his architect the great Sir Edwin Lutyens. The property, including the woodland on either side of the river, and Whiddon Park, is now in the hands of the National Trust and is open to the public. No-one who has a taste for the beautiful, the curious or the awe-inspiring should fail to visit Castle Drogo – it possesses all three qualities in ample measure.

Just beyond Hunter's Tor the path bends sharply to the right and begins to run NNW, away from the river. (There is a subsidiary path which goes straight on which would shorten our journey but it is so steep that it cannot be recommended.) After about a quarter of a mile we go through a gate and emerge into a farm road. Here we turn left and follow the road which goes downhill to the ancient and beautiful farm named Coombe but, having crossed a cattle-grid, we diverge to the left on a track which skirts round the farm. This takes us down to the river.

(If we were to turn right here we would, in half a mile, emerge upon the A382 at Dogmarsh Bridge, where we could go left for the Mill End Hotel or right for the Sandy Park Inn. This would entail retracing our steps back to this spot for our return to Fingle Bridge. If we decide to go to Dogmarsh Bridge we would follow a path through a series of small fields, and cross a tiny brook in the process. Here we would be quite close to the river, and would notice that it is quite unlike a normal Dartmoor river, being broad and comparatively slow flowing and enclosed by low banks.)

Following the Fisherman's Path downstream from the point where we came down from Coombe Farm, almost immediately we see ahead of us an iron footbridge spanning the river. The bridge gives access to Whiddon Park which lies to the south but we continue on the northern side of the stream. At about this point the character of the river begins to change. It is now flowing through a deep, narrow and rocky gorge and then falls over a weir into the deep pool below. Our path is now close to the water's edge and on our left hand we have the massive rocky pile of Hunter's Tor which stands within a few yards of the stream.

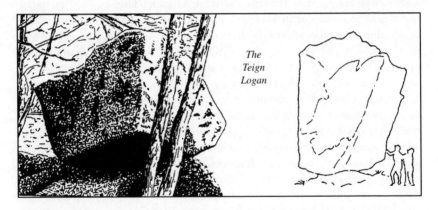

The Teign Logan

A little to the east of Hunter's Tor there is a tiny rocky island in the bed of the stream. Associated with this island is the famous Teign Logan or rocking stone. Samuel Rowe describes this rock in his *Perambulation of the Ancient & Royal Forest of Dartmoor,* published in 1848. He says that the stone is 7$\frac{1}{2}$ feet tall at its highest point and 10 feet 6 inches long by 7 feet 8 inches at its widest. He says that the stone can be made to rock perceptibly but only very slightly by the application of a man's strength and he is sure that it was used by the Druids to emphasise their power and overawe their adherents. Personally, I have never been able to make it rock at all – perhaps I pushed it in the wrong place.

We now continue along the footpath by the river and soon come abreast of Sharp Tor which is similar in many ways to Hunter's Tor which we passed earlier. The river scenery is now magnificent and in places we may find our attention wandering from the rocky and sometimes tricky path along which we are making our way.

At a point about a mile below Sharp Tor the river widens out considerably and here another weir has been constructed at a bend in the river. This is connected with the salmon and trout fishing which goes on there. The fishing is of course private. Now the gorge of the river is rather wider than has been the case so far and just beyond the weir the valley opens up even more and then we see ahead of us the bridge where we began our walk. What a sight it is! On our right the steep hillside, densely wooded, sweeps down almost to the water's edge. On the left the high ground has fallen back and a little lateral valley comes in from the north to meet the river. A tiny stream flows down this valley and falls into the Teign almost at the foot of one of the most venerable and beautiful bridges in Devon.

If we take the wide level track on the right beyond the toilets we shall come to the site of Fingle Mill. The remains of the miller's house stand by the track, and nearby is another ruined building, and an emplacement which has clearly at one time housed a water wheel. The mill was for grinding corn and was strategically placed near the bridge so as to catch the custom from both sides of the river. The mill was burned down about the turn of the century, and was never rebuilt.

If we hunt about a bit we may find one or two large iron collars. These formed the hub which took the axle and upon which the spokes of the water-wheel were mounted. They bear the name of the local mill-wright who made them – "Dicker, Chagford". It seems that the miller, or his wife, were early forerunners of the Angler's Rest as one of the old writers refers to the very indifferent refreshments he had at the mill-house when he visited Fingle Bridge. Later there was a little tea-house with a tea at 2d. a cup and postcards at a penny.

EXPLORATION 10. Widecombe village, Dunstone, Venton, Rugglestone Rock, Widecombe Hill, Bonehill Rocks, Bonehill Down, Bell Tor, Chinkwell and Honeybag Tors, Natsworthy Valley.

(CLEAR OF ALL FIRING AREAS)

Starting place:

Widecombe-in-the-Moor. Map reference 718768.

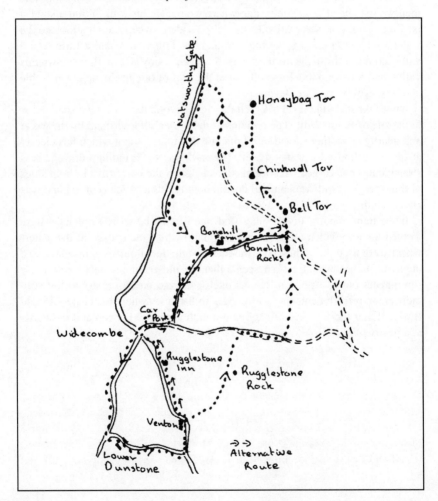

Approach:

From Torquay, Newton Abbot, etc. via Ilsington and Haytor, turning right at Hemsworthy Gate.

From Okehampton, Chagford, Moretonhampstead, Exeter, etc. via Bovey Tracey, then by way of B3387 Haytor road.

From Plymouth via A38 to Ashburton, leaving the town by North Street, turning left over Great Bridge, right in 2 miles at Ausewell Cross to Hemsworthy Gate, 3 miles further on, then left to Widecombe.

Amenities:

Cafes, Post Office and shops, public houses (the Old Inn and the Rugglestone) and toilets at Widecombe-in-the-Moor.

Parking for the exploration:

Large car park at starting place.

Type of excursion:

Easy moorland walking with some lanes and tracks. Two fairly stiff climbs of no great length. About 5 miles the round trip.

As we enter the village we see the church on our left and car park, toilets and cafe on the right, behind the green. Obviously, we cannot visit Widecombe without having a look at its famous and beautiful church, but to get into the church we have to pass round it and as we do so we notice the village sign. This consists of a sculptured representation of Uncle Tom Cobley and company astride the grey mare, the whole mounted on a granite pedestal. The sign was presented to the village by a local resident and benefactor to replace the original which was lost after it had been removed during the last war. Beyond the sign is a long two-storeyed granite building and here one road turns to the left and another goes off round the green to the right. The latter is the Natsworthy Valley road. We turn to the left however and then see that the road opens out into a little square flanked by the granite building just mentioned, the lych gate giving access to the church and a few cottages and shops, all built in granite.

This is a most charming spot to one who loves old Devonshire villages. More or less in the centre of the square are two ancient trees, one occupying the plinth where the village cross once stood. The long building on the north of the square was formerly the Church House, where the village bread was baked and the village ale brewed. It is now owned by the National Trust and among other uses serves as the village hall. The Old Inn stands to the west of the square and the former vicarage, Post Office and various shops are nearby. In the south-east corner of the square a narrow lane goes off and along this, about 250 yards distant, is the Rugglestone Inn.

It is not my intention to describe Widecombe church in detail, merely to say enough to encourage explorers to visit it. In brief it is magnificent in its simplicity. Its tall and stately tower and spacious interior both pay tribute to the genius of its builders. The condition in which it is kept speaks volumes as to the loving care lavished upon it by those who look after it.

Widecombe Church

Note particularly the wooden tablets fixed to the wall just inside the church. They tell the story of the events of Sunday, 21st October, 1638, when a tremendous thunderstorm broke out overhead during evensong. The church was struck by lightning and four people were killed and many injured. This event is the basis for the folk story which tells us how the Devil visited Widecombe that afternoon to seize a certain tinner who had failed to honour an obligation. The storm broke while these events were taking place and His Satanic Majesty rode off across the Moor with the tinner across his saddle. The tinner was holding a pack of cards as he sat in church and he dropped these on the floor of the valley below Warren House Inn. The aces of the pack can still be seen today – the walls of a collection of little fields called The Devil's Playing Cards.

Just outside the South Door of the church is the ancient churchyard cross, pieced together and restored after being found distributed around the church-yard in a number of fragments.

On leaving the church we take the road which runs south out of the village, noting as we go the village well, a tiny walled and roofed construction on the right of the road. This used to be the village water supply – today's supply is more wholesome but less interesting! A little over half a mile out of the village we reach a turning point on the left at a place called Dunstone. We turn into the lane and find that ahead of us, near a farm on the left and an ancient house (Dunstone Court) on the right, is a small patch of greensward. Upon this is a large rounded granite boulder, which seen from some angles has something of the appearance of a sleeping elephant.

This is the Rent Stone. Examination of the stone will reveal a number of shallow saucer-like depressions on the upper surface. It is said that here in medieval times, when the Black Death was at its height, the Lord of the Manor used to collect the rents from his tenants. The saucer shaped depressions were filled with vinegar and in them was placed the rent in the shape of coins which the vinegar was presumably intended to disinfect. The custom – minus the vinegar I imagine – is said to have been re-introduced by a Lord of the Manor with an antiquarian turn of mind in the 19th century. The ancient Dunstone Cross, restored in 1981 by another local benefactor, also stands upon the green.

We now leave the green, noting the ancient manor house as we go, and pass on southward along the lane for about a quarter of a mile when we come to a "T" junction where we turn left. About 300 yards further on we reach Venton, a cluster of farms and cottages among which we shall see a tiny building, obviously a church or chapel, though no longer used as such. This was built for Beatrice Chase, the well-known writer, whose home was at Venton for many years. She had been brought up in London, in the Catholic faith, and had become a nun at the age of 21. She came to Venton in about 1900 and had the chapel built in 1908 when she was 34.

At Venton a narrow lane goes off on the right near a farm and this in turn gives access to a footpath. This takes us through a couple of little fields and then brings us to the open moor. Here we turn left, away from the path, and follow the field walls round to the north. Soon ahead of us and to the left we see a low pile of rocks on the open common. This is Rugglestone Rock which is mentioned in Eden Phillpotts' novel *Widecombe Fair*. It is said that at one time two of the great slabs of rock were logan stones, that is they could be made to oscillate by bodily pressure. One of these logans was calculated to weigh 115 tons. It seems likely that formerly the Rugglestone was of greater local importance than is now the case. Perhaps it was a place at which local people met away from the eye of authority; but this is mere conjecture and nothing seems to be known about it now.

From the Rugglestone we turn to the NE and make our way across the common to the road up Widecombe Hill, which we should aim to strike just above the enclosures of Southway Farm. On reaching the road we turn right and continue along the road until we come to the end of the enclosures on our left. This point is reached just beyond a moorland lane leading down to a house called Sheena Tower. We now strike north across the common, walking along the contours as far as possible and find ourselves at Bonehill Rocks (locally called Bunnel Rocks), a small but interesting tor with several rock sculptures (entirely natural) which demand examination. But the great feature of the place is the splendid opportunity it affords for viewing the countryside around. From the tor the whole of the vale of Widecombe can be seen spread out below; the patchwork of little fields, open moorland, scattered cottages, winding streams and ancient church provide us a scene of such beauty as to baffle description. Having gazed our fill we cross a road which comes from the direction of Hemsworthy Gate. We find that a hundred yards or so beyond the rocks the road goes through a gate and disappears down a steep hill. Near the gate a rough track goes off to the north, along the steep hillside. Above us, on the summit of the hill stands Bell Tor, about 150 yards away. If we hunt about a little we shall find a well used path which we follow and which soon brings us, somewhat out of breath, to the rocks of Bell Tor. This we find provides an even better viewpoint than did Bonehill Rocks and we take advantage of this while regaining our breath.

We now continue northward and find that beyond Bell Tor we are faced with another, Chinkwell Tor, which lies beyond the saddle about 400 yards away. On reaching Chinkwell, which stands at over 1500 feet above sea-level, we find that it provides a breathtaking view of the eastern flank of Hameldown, the great whale-backed ridge which extends northward for some miles beyond Widecombe. About a quarter of a mile away to the north we see the rocks of Honeybag Tor, occupying a position on the same ridge but at a slightly lower altitude. The rocks of this tor are more massive and less scattered than those of Chinkwell.

We can if we wish and if we have time, make our way to Honeybag, at the same time conjecturing about its strange name. The authors of *The Place*

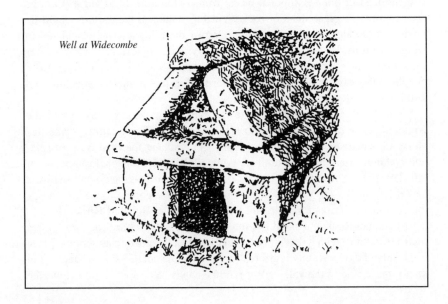

Well at Widecombe

Names of Devon do not hazard an opinion and I have nothing to offer myself, but William Crossing does make a tentative suggestion that the name may be related to *Hunne-bed,* a name given to the ancient burial monuments in parts of the Netherlands. There is no shortage of such monuments on Dartmoor.

It is now necessary to descend the steep hillside to the west. This will need some care and if we have extended our walk to Honeybag it may be as well to retrace our steps a couple of hundred yards or so, so as to take advantage of the more moderate slopes nearer Chinkwell Tor. Half-way down the slopes we reach an unmetalled road or track running north and south and turn right along it. (If we were to turn left here it would bring us back to Bonehill Rocks in about three-quarters of a mile.) Following the track along we soon come to a gate and passing through find that the track has become a lane – Thorneyhill Lane – and a very rough and steep one at that. It is not very long however and soon brings us to a surfaced road where we turn left. This is the Natsworthy Valley road, which extends from Widecombe along the eastern foot of Hameldon for over two miles. We are now walking along a narrow lane with woods and enclosures on either side.

After about three-quarters of a mile the road passes over a bridge spanning the East Webburn River. Just beyond the bridge the road makes an abrupt right turn and here, on the corner on the left, a path goes off across a field. We turn into this path and follow it along for about 300 yards when it enters a narrow lane between walls. This in turn brings us to another road, running steeply downhill from left to right. We turn right and continue downhill for about half a mile, passing one or two cottages as we go. At the end of the lane we come to a "T" junction and turning right find ourselves at the foot of Widecombe Hill, entering the village itself.

Please note: In a wet period it may be that the ground in the vicinity of the footpath leading from Venton towards the Rugglestone is very wet and marshy. If this is found to be the case it might be advisable to omit the visit to the Rugglestone. An alternative route would be to return to Widecombe village by the road leading from Venton past the Rugglestone Inn. On reaching the green take the right-hand road but instead of continuing up Widecombe Hill the first lane on the left is taken, just before the bridge is reached. This will take us past Bonehill Villa (we will come down this road later) and past the Bonehill farms to the moor gate near Bonehill Rocks.

Unfortunately there is no public right of access to the Rugglestone via the Rugglestone Inn. It can of course be reached from the open common above by approaching from the road down Widecombe Hill, via the wide corridor between the enclosures half-way down the hill.

EXPLORATION 11. Princetown, Nun's Cross, Plym Ford, Broad Rock, Erme Pits, Blacklane Brook, Ducks' Pool, Fox Tor, Childe's Tomb.

(CLEAR OF ALL FIRING AREAS)

Starting place:
Princetown. Map reference 589733.

Approach:
From Tavistock by way of B3357.
From Plymouth and Yelverton by way of B3212.
From Torquay and Newton Abbot via Bovey Tracey, Manaton, following signs towards Moretonhampstead, then B3212.
From Exeter, Chagford and Moretonhampstead by way of B3212.

Amenities:
All amenities at Princetown.

Parking for the exploration:
Car park behind the High Moorland Visitor Centre.

Type of excursion:
About 14 miles, the longest walk in the book. Not an expedition to be undertaken without proper preparation or in anything other than settled weather unless in the company of an experienced guide and it would be wise to set apart a whole day for its accomplishment. Typical moorland walking, no very steep gradients. In places the ground may be marshy underfoot.

The final expedition in my last book *Exploring Dartmoor,* was a visit to Cranmere Pool. This spot, deep in the heart of the peat morasses of northern Dartmoor, is often thought of and indeed in some senses is, the Mecca of Dartmoor explorers. This is because of its remoteness and the difficulty that inexperienced walkers sometimes have in finding the place; but most of all Cranmere Pool is famous because of the publicity it has received over a period of more than a century, ever since the Dartmoor Guide of the day, James Perrott, put it on the map about 1850 by conducting visitors to the pool who then left their visiting cards in a bottle provided for the purpose to prove their presence.

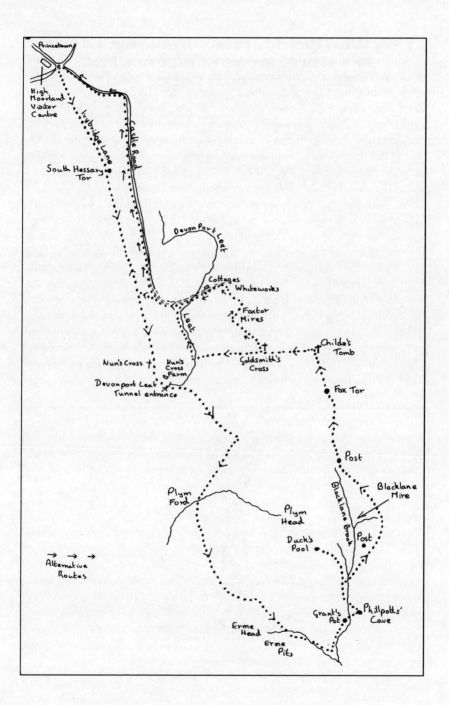

Princetown

High
Moorland
Visitor
Centre

Ivybridge Lane

Castle Road

South Hessary
Tor

Devonport Leat

Cottages
Whiteworks

Foxtor
Mires

Leat

Childe's
Tomb

Nun's Cross †

Nun's
Cross
Farm

Goldsmith's
Cross

Devonport Leat
Tunnel entrance

Fox Tor

Post

Blacklane
Mire

Plym
Ford

Blacklane Brook

Plym
Head

Duck's
Pool

Post

→ → →
Alternative
Routes

Grant's
Pot

Phillpotts'
Cave

Erme
Head

Erme
Pits

83

To give southern Dartmoor its due however, it should be said that in its barren interior there exists a spot at least as remote as and in some ways far more interesting than Cranmere Pool. This is Ducks' Pool, which lies about 4 miles SE of Princetown and a little less than a mile NNE of the source of the River Erme. The walker should not however take the distances quoted above too literally; it is seldom possible to pursue a straight course on Dartmoor for very long and seeking objects of interest often involves a considerable detour, even if the state of the ground does not force it upon one. Even so, if we take the route suggested here we will find a large variety of objects to interest us and at the end of the day will have covered about 14 miles.

We start the expedition from the square in Princetown. Crossing the Yelverton-Two Bridges road we go alongside the Plume of Feathers, through a gate, and then follow a track which mounts the rise to the SSE. This is Ivybridge Lane, along which released prisoners were once taken to start their long walk across the moor to Ivybridge Station. The track follows a cornditch wall past South Hessary Tor, on which there is a metal post marking the boundary of the Forest of Dartmoor, and subsequently passes other boundary marks related to the Forest and to the Burrator Reservoir water catchment area.

The wall turns away to the left, but we continue ahead, along a well-marked path, and nearly 2½ miles from Princetown come upon a massive stone cross. This is Nun's Cross, which is known to have been in existence in the year 1240, serving both as a boundary post and as a way marker on routes across

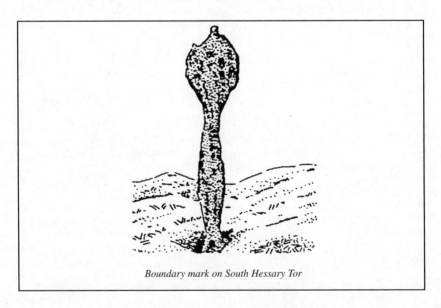

Boundary mark on South Hessary Tor

the moor which are reputed to have been used by the monks of Buckfast and Tavistock Abbeys in medieval times. The most familiar name related to these routes is the "Abbots' Way"; there is another route, which I have named the "Monks' Path", here coincident with the Abbots' Way, marked by a long series of stone crosses. Whatever the authenticity of these names the track we are joining is certainly very ancient.

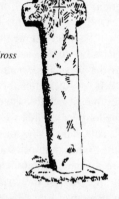

Nun's Cross

Nearby is Nun's Cross Farm, no longer a farm, the house being used as an adventure training centre by Royal Naval youth organisations. Down below the right-hand wall of the farm the track takes us past the entrance of the Devonport Leat tunnel, and follows the leat to where it is spanned by a foot bridge.

We do not cross the bridge, however, but turn away to the SE and follow the track for well over half a mile in this direction. The track, which in places is well marked but less so in others, now makes a sharp turn to the right and pursues a south-westerly course for another half mile or so. All this time the ground has been rising but when we are about a mile from Nun's Cross Farm we find that we have reached a sort of plateau which lies on the hillside to the west of the summit of Crane Hill. We now begin to descend into the valley we can see ahead of us to the south, the valley of the River Plym. We come down to the river among some very broken ground, which has clearly received the attention of the old tin-miners. Our track is well marked however and it leads us directly to a fording place on the river – Plym Ford on the map. Here we cross the river, in ordinary conditions without difficulty. Even when the river is in spate it is possible to cross quite near the ford without getting wet feet.

At Plym Ford we embark upon the final stage of our outward journey. Having crossed the river we mount the high ground to the south and follow the track, here quite well marked. Gradually we find that the track is veering to the left so that we keep rising ground on the east (left) and falling ground to the west. Here and there the track becomes somewhat confused and sometimes disappears altogether. However we have our compass with us and as long as we keep on a course a trifle to the east of south we cannot go far wrong. At a distance of rather more than a quarter of a mile from the ford we see ahead of us and just to the left of the track a cairn of stones – a ruined cist (a Bronze Age burial place) also lies nearby. Leaving the cairn on the left, the track now veers more decisively to the SE and for a short distance runs almost due east.

The going is better here and consequently the track is less easy to discern. Lying on the open moorland hereabouts are a number of large boulders and granite slabs.

One of these, to the left of the track, is Broad Rock. This is a well known local boundary stone, marking as it does the boundary between the Forest of Dartmoor to the east and the Parish of Cornwood and the Manor of Blatchford to the west and south. The rock bears the inscriptions "Broad Rock" and "B.B." – the latter means Blatchford Bounds. From Broad Rock the track resumes its south-easterly course. We are now going steadily downhill towards the long valley that we have seen ahead of us for some time.

This is the valley of the River Erme which rises at a spot called Erme Head just to the south of us as we descend. As we approach the stream we find that we are now among some very extensive tin workings. These extend to the further side of the river and consist of a collection of great pits and gullies which cover several acres. This area is known collectively as Erme Pits and is so marked on the map. The workings here are among the most spectacular on Dartmoor, but very little is known about them.

There is an ancient record however which indicates that tin was being won hereabouts as long ago as 1538 and there is another reference to the area in 1672. By the look of the place it could well have taken a century and a half to produce the great excavations here. To my mind it is astounding that men equipped with the primitive equipment available in those far off days could achieve such results.

The track again becomes rather confused as we approach the river but as we can clearly see Erme Pits ahead of us this matters little. The thing to avoid is the large marshy area round the head of the river and this is easily achieved by aiming directly for the pits; if deviation is necessary then it should be to the left.

Time has softened the effects of man's activities and the river banks in the vicinity of Erme Pits provide a fine spot for a rest and picnic. Here the tiny river comes down from its source in a series of little cataracts; there is a large area of rushes nearby and these features together with the backcloth provided by the old working now clothed in grass combine to make a peaceful and beautiful scene.

Refreshed by rest and food we now continue our exploration. We follow the river downstream a little further and pick our way through the tinners' debris which is strewn all around us. A search among the debris may reveal the scanty ruins of a building – probably a tinners' shelter. But whether we find this or not we cannot fail to notice the piles and built up banks of boulders all around. These banks are known as tinner buries, and this was their way of disposing of the mass of waste rock among which the tin-ore lay concealed.

At one time – as late as the 16th century – the tinners disposed of their waste by tipping it into any convenient stream which happened to be nearby. This got them into trouble, however, because the swift running Dartmoor rivers carried the debris far downstream and there were complaints that the harbours of Plymouth and Dartmouth were in danger of becoming choked by it. A bitter dispute resulted which eventually involved not only a local member of Parliament, Richard Strode, but also Parliament itself, plus the Stannary Parliament and the Stannary Courts. Strode was even imprisoned at Lydford Castle for a time by order of the Stannary Courts, but eventually sense and reason prevailed, hence the tinners' buries to be found in such numbers on the banks of almost every Dartmoor stream.

From Erme Pits Ford, which lies adjacent to the pits themselves, we strike south-east and after only about 400 yards of fairly rough going among the tinners' debris, we find ourselves on the bank of another stream which flows towards us from the left (north). This is the Blacklane Brook, whose proper name, now almost forgotten, seems to be the Wollake. Here we turn to the north and walk up-stream, with the stream on our right hand. This is another splendid example of a Dartmoor stream. It flows through a narrow rocky valley and after recent rain it is beautiful to behold as it rushes along foaming and bubbling in its rocky bed and over and around the great boulders which lie along its course.

But we must have eyes for other things besides natural beauty and we will be well rewarded in this valley if we pay attention to our surroundings. Signs of the ancient tinners are everywhere to be seen and soon we find one of their buildings, tucked into the high bank on the left of the river. This little building is of course roofless and ruinous. It is only about 18 feet long by about 7 feet wide. To me it is typical of the kind of building that working tinners used to build for their own shelter. I can see nothing to suggest that it was a blowing house, i.e. a smelting house. If at this point we mount the high ground to the west and hunt about we may find an elusive feature called Grant's Pot. This is a tiny rocky cave lying at the bottom of a small grassy hollow. The entrance is rather narrow, but a reasonably agile person can get inside without too much difficulty. Inside there is room for only about two persons, who would be very uncomfortable, but for some years the cave has been the site of a Dartmoor letter box, established by the Dawlish Scouts. The visitor may like to enter their name in the visitors' book and utilise the rubber stamp as a memento of their visit.

Leaving Grant's Pot (if we succeed in finding it) we now return to the stream and take the first opportunity of crossing to the other side. Here we mount the high ground above the bank and continue to walk northward. Soon we see a group of very large slabs of granite ahead of us and close to the stream. Close examination of these will bring to light another much larger cave, formed by the great slabs and blocks of granite of which the pile is composed. The entrance of the cave – a natural formation – has been partly closed up by building a dry stone wall on either side of the entrance. Inside there is room for half a dozen people to shelter. Locally the cave is called Phillpotts' Cave. It is said to be named after a certain Tony Phillpotts who was a servant of the local hunt many years ago. He is said to have been responsible for looking after the liquid refreshment required by the hunt when hounds met in this part of Dartmoor and the cave was his hiding place. This may well be true, but to my mind the original users of the cave are much more likely to have been the old tinners, who probably adapted it as a shelter or cache, or both.

On leaving Phillpotts' Cave it will be as well to cross the brook again as soon as possible. We then continue northward and after a few hundred yards come to a spot where the little stream comes together again after having flowed round a long island in its course. We keep to the left of the island and soon come to a little tributary, but almost immediately see before us, between the two streams, another tinners' building. Nearby but on the other (west) side of the stream are indications of another building. These buildings are quite ruinous but near the westernmost one lies a stone with a well worn semi-circular groove in it which was probably the bearing for the axle of a wheel or pulley. In view of this and other indications it seems likely that this was the site of a blowing house. It is known that such a building existed hereabouts in the first half of the 16th century.

Duck's Pool

We now continue to follow the little tributary stream through a veritable wilderness of tinners' works, among which we shall find yet another building, very small but equipped with a highly functional fireplace. Just beyond this we mount a bank and see Ducks' Pool before us. This is a large shallow hollow which may at some time have held a sheet of water. There is no such pool there today however, at the most nothing more than a large puddle. The hollow is very boggy and only in a dry season can it comfortably be crossed from side to side. Generally speaking it is best to go right round the pool, where there is more or less firm ground all the way.

Lying close to the western bank of the pool we shall see a large granite boulder. On reaching this we find a bronze plaque fastened to the boulder. This announces that the plaque was erected in memory of William Crossing, author of *Guide to Dartmoor,* who died in 1928. The plaque and the letter box, which will be found nearby, were inaugurated and are maintained by an organisation called Dobson's Moormen, based in Plymouth. The Ducks' Pool letter box is one of the oldest on the Moor, dating as it does from the early 1930s.

Having signed the visitors' book we now make our way back to Black Lane Brook; probably if the ground is anything other than quite dry it will be best to retrace our steps along the little tributary brook until we come to the main stream, where we cross to the eastern bank as soon as possible. We now climb to the high ground above the stream and turn to the north-east. Descending the opposite side of the hill we come to the south-eastern limit of Blacklane Mire. We cross over near the head of a little gully which runs up towards us from this flat marshy area and find a track which runs generally north-west along the eastern edge of the mire and then NNW parallel with the stream. The path and stream eventually converge and we join another track, which has come up the western bank and crosses the stream at this point. Formerly this route, known as Black Lane, was much used by the peatcutters to bring the peat in from the peat-ties. Nowadays it is used only by people like ourselves and farmers and hunters. The ground hereabouts is marshy, especially after prolonged rain but the track itself is quite firm.

Fox Tor Mire

The ground rises steadily to the north, and mounting a rise we see ahead what seems to be a wooden post sticking up in front of us. On reaching this it turns out to be, somewhat incongruously, an old railway sleeper; this we find marks the end of our track but ahead of us we now see a long deep gully which continues in the direction we want to go. The gully, which gets wider and deeper as we proceed, is Fox Tor Gert, an old miners' working. We follow it along as it goes northwards and now we can see, on the high ground ahead, the rocks of Fox Tor itself. We descend into the bottom of the gully and having crossed a little stream rise again on the other side and soon reach Fox Tor.

Childe's Tomb

This tor is not particularly impressive but standing as it does at an altitude of about 1400 feet above sea level it provides good views of the desolate heart of southern Dartmoor. In particular, ahead of us to the north and NW lies Fox Tor Mire, that famous Dartmoor bog and immediately in front of us on the further side of the wall that bounds the old Fox Tor newtake, we see Childe's Tomb, scene of an ancient tragedy, perhaps entirely legendary, perhaps partly true, which shall be recounted presently. On looking round the rocks of Fox Tor it may be that we shall find in a crevice among them a metal box containing the usual equipment to be found in a Dartmoor letter box. So many of these boxes have been vandalised in recent times that it is never certain that a particular one will be where we expect to find it. This one however has survived longer than many others.

A choice of routes now lies before us. If we wish to cut the journey short or if the ground is very wet the best choice on leaving Fox Tor is to steer down

Sheep Leap (Whiteworks)

the rocky hillside below the tor. The black Mine Cottages above Whiteworks are in full view from the Tor, as is the Devonport Leat. The leat is seen as a black line just below the skyline about a mile away to the NW. If we cannot make a bee-line for this we can at least take a reasonably direct route and so finish our walk along the good ground by the leat. As we walk along the Devonport Leat the observant rambler will notice that at intervals along the leat spurs of granite jut out from opposite sides of the stream in such a way as to suggest that some sort of bridge has existed here at some time. These are not bridges however, they are what are called locally "sheep leaps". They are provided so that sheep may have the use of grazing ground on either side of the stream. These animals quickly become adept at leaping from a spur to one on the opposite side of the leat. It is something to see (and to hear the baa-ing that goes on) as a flock, led by the bellwether, assembles in the vicinity of one of these sheep leaps and then one by one, makes the crossing en route to their nightly lair on higher ground.

Supposing however that we have time to spare when we leave Fox Tor or are anxious to visit Childe's Tomb we now descend the hillside to the north and pass through a hunting gate close to the monument. This we find to be a rude granite cross raised upon a pedestal which surmounts a stone chamber beneath the ground and partly surrounded by a circle or kerb of granite blocks. Other stones lie around, one of which is clearly part of the original socket stone for the cross. Only part of this monument is original: the cross itself, for example, was made for the purpose when the tomb was restored in the 19th century. Beneath the cross is a rectangular chamber which some authorities have described as a kistvaen but whether this is really the case is open to doubt. It is also doubtful whether, despite its name, anyone was ever buried here. Certain it is that the monument was destroyed early in the 19th century so that the stones might be used in connection with the building of Fox Tor Farmhouse, the ruins of which are nearby.

The best known version of the legend of Childe's Tomb has it that the principal character in the drama was one Amyas Childe of Plymstock, who is said to have lived in the reign of Edward III – i.e. in the 14th century. The legend says that Childe was out hunting one day when the party was overtaken by bad weather. Childe became separated from his companions and knowing himself to be lost and in danger of death from exposure he killed his horse and having disembowelled it crept inside the carcass for shelter. He froze to death however, but before he died he wrote his will – in blood of course – leaving his estate of Plymstock to whichever church gave his body burial. The legend goes on to say that some men (or perhaps monks) from Tavistock found the body and were conveying it back to Tavistock Abbey for burial when they learned that a plot was afoot to take the body from them so that it might be buried elsewhere. This danger was overcome by a strategem however – the monks threw a bridge across the River Tavy just outside Tavistock where no bridge had been before and the body was safely smuggled into the Abbey and buried there, the estate of Plymstock coming into possession of the monks of Tavistock as a result.

This version of the legend was first reduced to writing by Tristram Risdon in his *Survey of the County of Devon,* completed about 1630 but not published until 1714. Thomas Westcote also repeats the legend in his *View of Devonshire.* This seems to have been completed about 1630 also, but did not reach the printer until 1845. In 1946, however, Professor H.P.R. Finberg published the result of his own research into the facts behind this legend.

Briefly, Professor Finberg discovered that the hero of this drama was probably one Ordulf, son of Ordgar, the Saxon Earl of Devon. (The name Childe is probably derived from Cild – a Saxon title of honour meaning "the young lord".) It seems that it was Ordulf who lost his way and perished in the manner described in the legend. He had already made his will in which he left one of his manors – Antony in Cornwall – to the church where he should be buried and this manor eventually came into the possession of the monks of Tavistock. It is known that Ordulf was alive in 1066 and that the Manor of Plymstock was already in possession of the monks of Tavistock at that time, having been left to them by one

Goldsmith's Cross

Eadwig, brother of King Edmund Ironside, who died during the reign of Canute.*

From the foregoing it will be seen that the legend of Childe the Hunter is much older than used to be thought and that it is unlikely that the hero was ever buried beneath the monument that bears his name.

On leaving Childe's Tomb we take a westerly course – there is usually a well marked path – running parallel with the boundary wall which we keep to on our left. This keeps us clear of the bog and brings us in about half a mile to Goldsmith's Cross, another granite cross set in a boulder. This ancient monument gets its name from the fact that having been lost for centuries it was eventually rediscovered by Lt. Goldsmith, R.N., in 1903 and was re-erected in its original socket in the boulder. This cross, together with Childe's Tomb and Nun's Cross and others nearby, marks the line of the old Monks' Path from Buckfast to Buckland and probably dates from medieval times. From the cross a track, marked by blobs of paint and occasional posts, runs in a north-westerly direction to Whiteworks. The track is usually reasonably passable with just one or two splashy places. If it is too wet for comfort however the difficulty can be got over by making a detour by way of the higher ground to the west and NW giving us the opportunity to walk along the Devonport Leat. Whichever way we go we will reach the road in the vicinity of Whiteworks.

We now turn left and follow the road until it reaches its highest point. Here the road is crossed by a track which comes up left, from the direction of Burrator, and goes down to the right towards Peat Cot, and we can choose the final part of our route. We can either cut across left (NW) to the track we set out on, and turning right retrace the first part of our excursion, or we can follow the road back to Princetown. Although this is a hard road, much of it is alongside open moorland, and it makes a very pleasant walk.

* A full and fascinating account of what Professor Finberg found out about this ancient legend can be read in Volume 78 of the *Transactions of the Devonshire Association (1946)*. The Devon Library Service has all these volumes which are available to the public.

EXPLORATION 12. Ringmoor Down, Gutter Tor, Ditsworthy Warren, Drizzle Combe, Plym Valley, Eylesbarrow, Burracombe Gate and a short walk to Sheeps Tor.

(CLEAR OF ALL FIRING AREAS)

Starting place:
Ringmoor Down, 1¹/₂ miles east of Sheepstor village, near ford over Sheepstor Brook. Map reference 578673.

Approach:
From Okehampton, Tavistock, etc. via A386 to Yelverton, there turning left at round-about then right in half a mile for Dousland and Sheepstor, by way of Burrator Lake.
From Exeter, Bovey Tracey etc. to Moretonhampstead then via B3212 by way of Two Bridges and Princetown. Turn left at Dousland, about 5 miles beyond Princetown and follow signposts to Burrator Lake and Sheepstor.
From Plymouth, etc. by way of A386 to Yelverton, then as above, turning right at roundabout.
From Torquay, Newton Abbot, etc. via A38 to Ivybridge, there turning right for Cornwood. By-passing Lee Moor village and Wotter, turn right at Beatland Corner to Cadover Bridge and thence to Meavy, after which follow signposts for Burrator and Sheepstor.

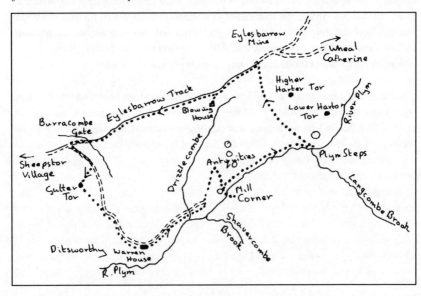

Amenities:

All amenities at Yelverton and Princetown. Post Office/shop and public house (Burrator Inn) at Dousland. Public house at Meavy (Royal Oak). Toilets near dam at Burrator Lake.

Parking for the exploration:

Limited space on edge of common clear of road at starting place.

Type of excursion:

Typical moorland walking, some tracks and paths. There is some tussocky grass and heather but not too much and very few steep climbs. About 7$^1/_2$ miles.

To reach our starting place we have driven from Sheepstor village for about a mile and a half along a narrow moorland road with open common on the right and field walls on the left. This road ends when it reaches the ford over the Sheepstor Brook, mentioned above. The road then becomes a moorland track, much used in former times by the old tin-miners but originally formed it seems along the western arm of the Abbots' Way, the track which is reputed to have been used by the monks when travelling between Buckfast and Buckland Abbeys. As we look around us we notice that less than a mile away to the NW stands the great bulk of Sheeps Tor, hiding from our view the waters of Burrator Lake which we saw as we approached our starting place. Only a quarter of a mile away and almost due south of us lies Gutter Tor and to the summit of this we now make our way, choosing the easiest route we can devise across the common.

Gutter is not one of Dartmoor's great tors but it is beautiful in its own way and commanding as it does the valley of the River Plym it provides a splendid vantage point. The vicinity of Gutter Tor is strewn with relics of the Bronze Age; hut circles, cairns and kistvaens can all be found within a few hundred yards of the tor but these are not among the most interesting of their kind and on this occasion we shall have to defer their examination. Once having reached the summit of Gutter we shall find that the tor is a low pile of rocks with nothing very spectacular about them.

There is an item of great interest here however. A few feet in front of the rocks at the SE edge of the tor will be found a rectangular slab of granite about 30 inches long by 22 inches wide and 5 inches thick, with two round holes each about an inch in diameter. The slab has been damaged in recent years. This is the upper stone – the lid in fact – of a vermin trap, used by the rabbit warreners to catch stoats and weasels which preyed upon their rabbits. The trap consisted of a chamber constructed from blocks of granite with the slab we see before us a lid. The trap was fitted with a sliding door which slid in grooves and was actuated by a pressure plate. The holes in the lid accommodated the wooden members which supported the cord or wire from which the sliding door was suspended. Many such traps are found in the vicinity of the Dartmoor warrens, most of them in a ruinous condition. Such traps have not been used in living memory; they probably date back to the 18th century.

Having examined the trap and admired the view, we make our way down the slope – there is a path if we can find it – in a south-easterly direction. At the foot of the hill we shall find a wide track running NW/SE. Here we turn right and follow the track for about 400 yards.

Soon we see ahead of us, tucked into the hillside, a house and outbuildings. In the vicinity and quite close to the track a number of low mounds of earth covered with grass will be found. These are the warreners' "buries" or burrows, the artificial lairs made by the ancient warreners to provide their rabbits with the kind of accommodation they like.

We now arrive at the house which we find to be a substantial dwelling built from granite and provided with a constant supply of fresh water from the nearby moor. This is Ditsworthy Warren House, the residence of the last practising warrener on Dartmoor. There were formerly five such warrens in the Plym valley. They all seem to have gone out of business during the present century but this was the one which survived the longest. It closed down during the early 1950s when the Rabbit Clearance Order made it an offence to "harbour" wild rabbits. Ditsworthy Warren is no longer a dwelling but it is in good condition and is used as an adventure training centre by youth

*Ditsworthy
Warren House*

organisations. The house and land – many hundreds of acres on both sides of the Plym – are owned by the National Trust. Adjoining the house is a tiny paddock surrounded on all sides by stone walls. Built into the walls of this paddock will be found three kennels, the homes of the warrener's dogs who were a very important part of his equipment. We usually discover when examining one of these old warren farms that special arrangements were made for the dogs. The Dartmoor warrener was much too frugal and sensible a person to waste money on powder and shot which in any case damaged the valuable meat and fur. Dogs and nets were both cheap and efficient.

From Ditsworthy Warren House we now turn north-east. We shall find a well marked path running along the hillside above the house and its attendant fields and this we follow. At first we have the field walls on our right and open moorland on the left, but the walls soon come to an end and then we see the River Plym flowing below us on the right about 200 yards away. At a point rather less than half a mile from the house the track we are following crosses a tiny stream which comes in from the north. Having crossed we stand for a moment and take stock of the situation. The stream we have just crossed is Thrushelcombe Brook, and the valley down which it flows is Thrushel Combe. Over the centuries this name had been corrupted into Drizzle Combe and this is now its generally accepted name.

Menhir – Drizzlecombe

Drizzle Combe is a wide shallow valley and in it is a complex of prehistoric remains of the Bronze Age of very great interest. The first of these we come to is a kistvaen in average condition and minus its coverstone. This lies near and to the left of the track close to the point where the track veers away to the

Kistvaen

97

right, en route for the river which it reaches at a ford. From the kistvaen we turn to the north and make our way towards three large standing stones which have been within our view for some time. On reaching them we find that each of the three stones stands at the head of a row of stones running NE/SW. At the opposite end of each row is a barrow, i.e. a burial place, once covered by a cairn of stones. One of the three great standing stones is the tallest on Dartmoor, over 14 feet in height. Nearby are other remains of the same prehistoric period, including hut circles and enclosed hut groups. There are also two more kistvaens, both in good condition, one of them a splendid specimen complete with cover stone, which has been moved to one side to exhibit the interior of the grave. Between the stone rows and the river will be found a very large cairn of stones with a depression in the centre. This is appropriately named the Giant's Basin.

From the Giant's Basin we turn towards the river and should strike it close to the spot where a tiny island lies in the river bed. Here, in normal conditions, we can cross the river. Having done so we find ourselves faced by a steep cliff and at the foot of this, between the cliff and the river, we see the scanty remains of a building. This place is Mill Corner and the building was Cole's Mill, a blowing house where tin was smelted by the old tin-miners. Lying among the ruins are two or three blocks of granite with saucer shaped depressions in them. These are mortar stones in which the tin ore was crushed before smelting. The building probably dates from the 17th century or a little later.

We recross the river and here we have to decide which route to take. If we decide that we wish to extend our excursion by a couple of miles we shall continue along the river upstream for about three-quarters of a mile, as far as Plym Steps. If not we make our way back to the Giant's Basin and the stone rows, then follow the valley and the stream NNE for about half a mile. Here, having passed one ruined building. we reach yet another quite close to the spot where the stream rises. This is the Eylesbarrow blowing house, an important place in the history of tin-mining on Dartmoor, as will be explained later.

Assuming that we are going to take the longer route, we now set off upstream along the Plym with the river on our right. The going is rough in places, being mostly tufty grass and heather, but not impassable or anything like it. After about three-quarters of a mile we reach a spot where a stream comes in from the right (south). The stream is the Langcombe Brook and the place is Plym Steps, but in case you expected to find stepping stones here prepare to be disappointed – there are none. There is a ford however and it is usually possible to cross here, with greater or lesser difficulty according to the state of the river. The ford serves the ancient track called the Abbot's Way mentioned earlier.

North-west of the river and quite close to it stands Lower Hartor Tor and beyond that Higher Hartor Tor. At the foot of Lower Hartor Tor will be found a prehistoric enclosure containing three hut circles. If we were to follow the Plym upstream for a couple of miles we would come to Plym Head, the source of the stream, one of the loneliest spots on southern Dartmoor. Between Plym Steps and Plym Head are the sites of two tinners' blowing houses and also the substantial remains of Wheal Catherine, an early 19th century tin-mine. South of the river, close to the Langcombe Brook many tinners' remains will be found including the ruins of what appear to have been buildings.

The fact is that this area is particularly rich in remains of various kinds and a whole day could easily be spent in exploring them, but not to-day alas; we must now turn for home. This we do by following the track which leads us away from Plym Steps in a north-westerly direction gradually veering to the north and finally emerging on the high ground with another track coming in from the north-east. In the vicinity of the junction of the two tracks a complex of ruined buildings will be seen. These are the ruins of the mine buildings and works associated with the Eylesbarrow mine; a farmhouse of comparatively modern date was also situated here.

Flue at Drizzlecombe Blowing House (Eylesbarrow Mine)

The name Eylesbarrow properly belongs to a group of tumuli on the summit of the hill about a quarter of a mile to the north of the mine building but it has come to be applied to the hill itself and thence to the mine. This was one of Dartmoor's most ancient tin-mines, dating back as it does to the 17th century or earlier. Among the many remains to be found here are ruined buildings which once housed the water wheels which powered the stamping mills and the pumping machinery.

Having examined the ruins we now take the main track and follow it downhill to the SW. Soon another track will be seen going off to the left. We take this and it brings us to a little valley close to the head of the stream which flows down Drizzle Combe. In the little dell are the ruins of a fair sized building among which are several very large worked blocks of granite. This is the Eylesbarrow blowing house referred to earlier. It is known that tin was being smelted here as recently as 1826, but it is clear from its construction that it was not one of the typically Dartmoor type of blowing houses but is of a type referred to as "reverberatory", using fuel more sophisticated and efficient than the charcoal or timber of the old tinners. A second building, also mentioned earlier, can be found a couple of hundred yards further down the little stream. This appears to have housed a set of stamps for crushing the ore before smelting.*

From the tinners' buildings we return to the main track and follow it down hill for a further mile. The going is now easy and the greensward beside the track springy. As we stride along it may be profitable to remember that, if all we are told is true, six hundred and more years ago the monks of Buckfast were making their way along this track, en route for Buckland Abbey, or vice versa. At the foot of the hill the track brings us to where there is a foot-bridge and a ford. This is the Sheepstor Brook and the name of the place is Burracombe Gate. A few yards away on the other side of the stream is the spot where we left our transport several hours ago, at the foot of Gutter Tor.

Explorers who decide to embark upon this excursion will inevitably come very close to or even pass through the beautiful old village of Sheepstor, which is really no more than a hamlet. So beautiful is it and so full of curiosities, both ancient and less ancient, that it would be a pity to pass it by without a glance. Old it certainly is, with a past buried deep in the roots of Devon history. Sheepstor is a parish in its own right and covers the area of the ancient manor of the same name. Its name is of course taken from the tor which overshadows the village. How that great rock got its name is uncertain, the earliest form

---

*A well researched account of the Eylesbarrow site including a description of the smelting house can be found in *The Industrial Archaeology of Dartmoor* by Helen Harris, published by Peninsula Press. The author also offers a possible explanation as to the purpose of the two double rows of stone posts to be found on the higher ground in the area.

Sheepstor

(1168) seems to have been Sitelestorra, which may have been derived from a person named Scyttel, or it may have been that the shape of the tor was thought to resemble a bar or bolt, in Old English *scyttel*. It is I think, safe to say that it had nothing to do with sheep and that we don't really know what it means.

The church is of course the focal point in the village. This is a typical Dartmoor church, built of granite and Roborough stone. The present building is largely 16th century in date but it stands upon a site probably first sanctified in Saxon or early Norman times. Just outside the churchyard, near the lychgate, is the village cross. Until 1910 this stood in a field nearby where, having had its arms knocked off, it did duty as a rubbing post for cattle. To commemorate King George V's coronation the cross was restored – two new arms were very cunningly fitted – and it was placed where it now stands, a splendid example of its kind. Having entered the churchyard through the lychgate the church itself stands ahead and to the left. To the right will be seen another old granite cross in fine condition standing by a stile at the head of a very long steep flight of stone steps. The cross acts as a hand-hold to help one over the stile, a very proper function for the symbol of Christianity one must agree. Where this cross came from originally seems to be unknown. It is said to have been placed it its present position early in the 20th century.

Beyond the church towards the eastern end of the churchyard will be seen a set of tombstones surrounded by iron railings, with a coat of arms upon a metal plaque attached to the railings. These are the tombs of four members of the Brooke family, the White Rajahs of Sarawak. The romantic story of how

James Brooke was adopted by the Rajah and people of Sarawak in western Borneo and how he was later made Rajah by their overlord the Sultan of Brunei is probably well known by many people.

Not so many people are aware that James Brooke and his successors made their English home at Sheepstor, nor that they are buried in the churchyard here. But here they lie and here they sleep until Judgment Day, three White Rajahs and the man who would have been the fourth had not history intervened and the British Empire become a thing of memory only.

Nuthatch

A road winds round the churchyard and then strikes off to the SE towards Ringmoor Down. Just outside the village a lane leaves this road on the left. This is a "no through road", but it leads to some farms and before reaching them runs along the side of the common at the foot of Sheeps Tor. There is space for parking off this road and the rocks are then only a few yards away. On a fine day a visit to the summit of the tor will be well repaid; the views from here are stupendous, especially to the west and north-west. Below lies Burrator Lake, reputedly the finest man-made lake in England, fringed as it is by trees and overshadowed by great rocky tors. Jutting out into the waters of the lake will be seen Longstone Island, not really an island but rather a peninsula.

Upon this thumb of land stand the ruins of Longstone, the ancient home of the Elford family, lords of the Manor of Sheepstor for centuries. It seems likely that the summit of Sheeps Tor was formerly the site of a beacon, to be lit in times of danger. There is a record of the early 17th century which implies that the residents of Sheepstor were exempted from some public duties and payments because of their responsibility for manning the beacon at Sheeps Tor.

As we descend from the tor we may if we have the time scrutinise the rocks facing the road in the hope of identifying the Pixies' Cave. This is said to have been a chamber capable of holding several people. In 1802 it was described as being six feet long, four feet wide and five feet high, and very difficult to find. Crossing says it was much smaller than that in his day

Goldcrest

because the rocks had shifted. He thought it inadvisable to attempt to enter the cave. Personally I have never been able to identify it but it was reputed to be the home of the pixies and also and more probably the hiding place in which a member of the Elford family sought refuge when "on the run" from the Roundheads during the Civil War.

Looking down upon the lake from the summit of the tor it will have become apparent that a serviceable road runs right round the lake. This is a truly beautiful scenic drive and a circuit of the lake will set the seal upon a day that has produced much of beauty, interest and curiosity which our exploration has far from exhausted.

EXPLORATION 13. Okehampton, Moor Gate, Black Down, High Willhays, Yes Tor.
(PARTLY WITHIN THE OKEHAMPTON FIRING AREA)

Starting place:
Beyond Moor Gate, near Okehampton Camp. Map reference 593927.

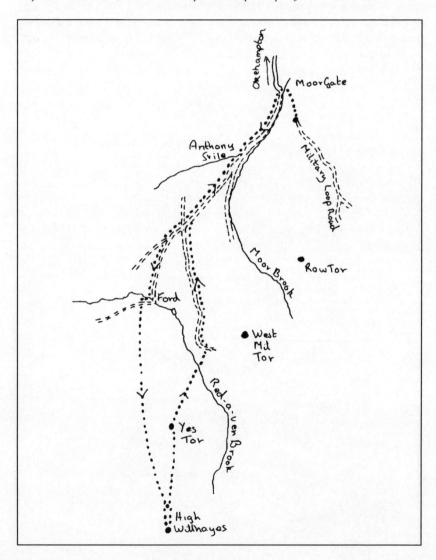

Approach:

To Okehampton from all directions. In the town turn south into George Street (the White Hart Hotel stands on the corner near the town centre). A little way along turn half right into Station Road and follow the road along, uphill and out of the town. About half a mile out of the town the road crosses the railway and turns east. A quarter of a mile further on it turns hard right across the open common and passes Fitz's Well where there is a stone cross to the right of the road and brings us to Okehampton Camp. The road skirts the camp and soon arrives at Moor Gate where it crosses the Moor Brook at a ford.

Parking for the exploration:

About 300 yards up the hill beyond the ford there is a smooth area on the right. This is our starting place.

Amenities:

All amenities at Okehampton.

Type of excursion:

High moorland, rocks and tors. Some rough tracks. Not an excursion to be attempted in any but settled weather unless an experienced guide is available. In any case there would be no point in embarking on this walk in conditions of bad visibility as the splendid views are one of the main attractions.

Check to make sure that there is no firing scheduled to take place on the Okehampton range. About 6 miles the round trip.

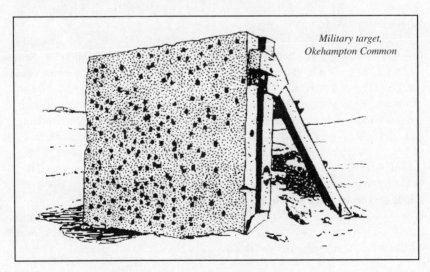

Military target, Okehampton Common

Having parked clear of the road we return to the stream and recross (there is a bridge as well as a ford) and walk along the tarmac road – once a rough moorland track – which runs southward, following the line of the brook. Although we have the camp and its enclosures on our right (west), ahead of us, as far as the eye can see we have open moorland dominated by a multiplicity of great tors, Row Tor, West Mill Tor and Yes Tor to name but a few. High Willhays is not in view and we shall not see it for some time. This wild country is networked by a system of military roads, many of them formed along the lines of much more ancient tracks. It is along one of these that we are now making our way.

The fact is that the Army has had much more than a foothold on Dartmoor for over a century. It was used as a training ground during the Napoleonic and Crimean Wars, but in the 1870s an annual camp was started and this went on until the 1890s when a permanent camp was set up. This is still with us. These military activities have been and still are the subject of bitter controversy, unsuitable for inclusion in a book like this. Suffice it to say that it is extremely difficult to reconcile the concept of a National Park with a permanent military presence, especially when the latter includes live artillery firing.

About a third of a mile from Moor Gate we come to a point called Anthony Stile. Who Anthony was is not apparent, but there is a stile in the wall a short distance to the right. We follow the tarmac road for another 200 yards and then fork right on a track which goes in a south-westerly direction. The land now begins to rise more steeply and at a point on Black Down (the name of the open moorland we are traversing) about a mile from Anthony Stile and having passed Row Tor away to our left, we come abreast of West Mill Tor which towers over 400 feet above us, also on our left.

There would be little point in climbing West Mill Tor unless we are really anxious to do so as we shall be ascending two even higher tors quite soon. This being so we pass it by and continue along the track as before until we reach a fork in the track. We still have Yes Tor in view to the south, that is half left from us. We go straight ahead, ignoring the left-hand track but a hundred yards or so further on come to another fork and here we go off to the left. Running parallel with our track (after it crosses the raised bank covering a water pipe-line – marked as a straight black line on the map) we can find on our left a long shallow trench which once accommodated a set of tramlines upon which a moving target ran backwards and forwards for use in firing practice. Our track brings us down into the valley of a little stream, the Red-a-ven Brook, which rises about a mile to the south of the foot of High Willhays. At the foot of the incline the track crosses the Red-a-ven at a ford. We could at this point, or a little earlier if we wished, climb the slopes of Yes Tor direct. But this is a really stiff climb and if we intend to complete the whole excursion the best course is not to do so but to defer the visit until a little later. So, we continue over the ford and leave the track, which has now turned to the west. We steer a course about SSW which takes us up a fairly steep slope, keeping the rocks of Yes Tor well to the left as we climb. This is a longish climb of about three-quarters of a mile. The going is good however and we shall soon find ourselves on the ridge with Yes Tor to the left and the rocks of High Willhays – the first time we have seen them – just coming into view ahead of us to the south.

Not only is High Willhays (always pronounced High Willys) a great and

Border Collie

Dartmoor Pony and Belted Galloways

impressive hill, the summit plateau being almost half a mile in length from north to south, but it is also Dartmoor's highest point. Indeed at 2039 feet above sea-level it is the highest land in England, south of the Pennines. As can be imagined, on a clear day the views to be obtained from its summit are spectacular, especially those of Dartmoor itself. About 600 feet below us to the south and west lies the valley of the West Okement River. At the bottom of this valley but out of view stand the tiny oaks of Black Tor Copse, one of Dartmoor's ancient dwarfed oakwoods. Above the trees and in full view are the rocks of Black Tor itself.

If we want a closer look at this valley we can have it without too much effort by descending the moderate slopes at the western end of High Willhays to the sloping platform provided by Fordsland Ledge, about 200 feet below the summit. From this vantage point the valley opens up and presents an entirely new field of vision including views into the innermost parts of the Forest, especially to the south. There is a cairn with a ruined kistvaen on the ledge.

From the summit of High Willhays – there is a Dartmoor letter box here if we care to search for it – we turn again to the north and make for the rocks of Yes Tor which lie across the shallow saddle from High Willhays, about half a mile away. Yes Tor is another of Dartmoor's great tors. At 2030 feet it is almost as high as High Willhays; its rocks are much more massive and impressive and the views from it are stupendous. Looking away from the Moor, we have the whole of North and West Devon and part of Somerset laid out before us. On a clear day we can see as far afield as Exmoor and the Bristol Channel and the patchwork of the countryside in between is indescribably beautiful. Immediately below us to the north the precipitous sides of Yes Tor slope down to the Red-a-ven Brook. The Fishcombe Water and the West Okement lie below us to the west, winding below those two great twins Longstone Hill and Homerton Hill. To the Dartmoor lover this is country whose beauty almost baffles description and the contemplation of which brings a lump into the throat. There is nothing like this to be seen anywhere else in Devon or in South-West England.

Beautiful though it is we must sooner or later leave Yes Tor – its name by the way is said to be a corruption of Ernestorre, meaning eagle's tor. There are no eagles there today, but plenty of buzzards. We leave the tor by making our way down the rocky hillside to the NNE, avoiding the steepest parts which lie to our right. This will bring us in about half a mile to the Red-a-ven Brook again. We should strike the stream at a point where it is flowing from NW to SE and here we cross the brook and continue due north for a short distance until we strike a rough track which comes down from the SE, i.e. from West Mill Tor. We turn left into this track and follow it as it goes northwards. We come to a cross-ways and turn right – NE. From here we follow our outward route reversed, and at a point about a mile and a half from the summit of Yes Tor, we reach Anthony Stile. Alternatively, instead of making for Anthony Stile we can strike across the common to the right and having crossed the Moor Brook at some convenient place follow it back to Moor Gate. The mile or so of springy turf makes a pleasant change from the stony tracks we have been using. (To take a short cut back to the starting place as we approach the ford may not be wise as there is a miry area extending from the right bank.)

EXPLORATION 14. Cadover Bridge, Wigford Down, the Dewerstone, Dewerstone Wood, Shaugh Bridge, West Down, North Wood.
(CLEAR OF ALL FIRING AREAS)

Starting place:
Cadover Bridge on River Plym, 2¹/₂ miles south of Meavy village. Map reference 555646.

Approach:
From Plymouth via Plympton and Shaugh Prior.
From Torquay and South Devon via A38 to Ivybridge then by way of Cornwood. By-pass Lee Moor village and Wotter, turning right at Beatland Corner.
From Tavistock, Okehampton, Exeter, Bovey Tracey, etc. to Princetown then via B3212 to Dousland turning left on to side road to Meavy Bridge and thence to Cadover Bridge.

Amenities:
All amenities at Princetown, Shaugh Prior and Cornwood. Post Office/shop and inn (Royal Oak) at Meavy.

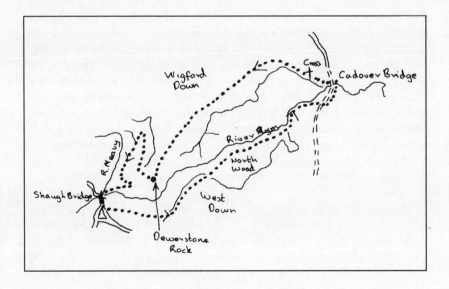

Parking for the exploration:
Ample parking space off the road in vicinity of Cadover Bridge.

Type of excursion:
Some open moorland but mostly footpaths and tracks. No very long steep climbs. Splendid riverside scenery. Some of the paths and tracks will be muddy after rain. About 5 miles the round trip.

Cross, Wigford Down

Our starting place for this excursion is Cadover Bridge where the road from Plympton to Yelverton crosses the River Plym. This area of Dartmoor is much involved with the china clay industry and there is evidence of this on every hand in the shape of the great mounds of silver sand separated from the kaolin in the process of refinement. Until very recently the road running SE from Cadover Bridge was the direct route between northern and western Dartmoor and Ivybridge, where it connected with the A38. Now the road is closed to general traffic from a point about a mile and a half SE of Cadover Bridge because of the increased activities of the china clay industry. Traffic has now to make a detour, taking the road running south from the bridge and skirting the village of Shaugh Prior. It is best to join or leave the A38 in the vicinity of Plympton.

Wherever we have parked we should make for the northern end of the bridge and make our way on to the common to the west. Here, about a hundred yards from the road, standing on rising ground will be found a tall granite cross. This cross seems to have no proper name and is always referred to as the cross on Wigford Down. It is one of several in the vicinity, survivors from medieval times and marking the track across the Moor connecting Plympton Priory with some of the lands held by the monks on the western side of Dartmoor. It will be noticed that the cross has been damaged and repaired; in fact the lower part of the shaft is a replacement. The upper part of the cross was found nearby in the late 19th century and re-erected at what is thought to have been its original site.

From the cross we continue westward across the common – Wigford Down as we have learned from the name of the cross – keeping the farm enclosures on our left.

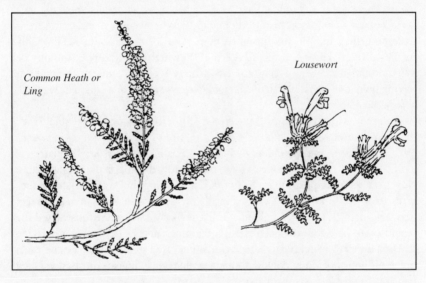

Common Heath or Ling

Lousewort

As we proceed we shall find that the wall varies its direction considerably, bearing first NW, then SW, then almost due south. There is no need for us to follow it slavishly however and if we bear away to the right – to the north that is – it may be that we shall come across a number of hut circles or even a kistvaen, lying among the quantities of surface rock with which the common is strewn. There are also a number of upright stones, running in a line across Wigford Down. These will be found to bear the letter "L" carved upon them. This indicates that they are boundary stones denoting the boundary of the estate of the Lopes family who have held this property for over a hundred and fifty years. The present head of the family is Lord Roborough, a former Lord Lieutenant of Devon, an office that he had held for many years.

Whatever we do in the way of local exploration our general intention is to follow the line of the enclosures and this will soon bring into view, about half a mile away to the SW, the rising ground of Dewerstone Hill. As the ground rises we stop from time to time to take in the view, especially to the north. Here we see some of the great tors of central and western Dartmoor, including Great Mis Tor, Great and Middle Staple Tors and Cox Tor among them. To the west lies the partly wooded valley of the Meavy, down which the river makes its way southward to join its big sister the Plym at Shaugh Bridge. The common across which we are walking is extensively littered with surface boulders and is intersected by long low banks of earth and stones – reaves is their Dartmoor name. These are found in many parts of the Moor and generally speaking they are accepted as being prehistoric boundaries. Whether this is the case here is uncertain; they may in this instance be part of a long abandoned, probably medieval farm. There is a record dated 1306 which refers to one Anthony de Wigworthie, from whom Wigford Down may well have taken its name, as having held land in the parish of Shaugh Prior. We are in that parish as we walk across the common.

We are now quite close to Dewerstone Hill, close enough to be able to see the low summit rocks. About 250 yards in front of the hill is a wide semi-circular bank of granite boulders which extends in an arc, nearly a quarter of a mile in length, from the edge of the woods below the hill on the south-eastern slopes, to a similar position on the west. On reaching this great bank of stones it resolves itself into two walls, one inside the other with a gap of about 9 feet between them. It has been calculated that if the walls were reconstructed the result would be two walls each about 5 feet thick and 12–13 feet apart. To the right of the path which leads into the area enclosed by the walls are the ruins of a building, apparently contemporary with the walls, but so confused are they that it is impossible to make anything of them.

Continuing up the hill we come, about 150 yards further on, to the low walls of another enclosure. On examination this turns out to be an incomplete rectangle. The south-eastern wall has been removed, probably to provide material for a more modern wall nearby. It seems likely that there never was a wall on the SW, the summit rocks of the hill serving instead. Inside this enclosure, incorporated with the wall at the northern corner, is a fair sized hut circle. This very interesting site has been interpreted as being a Bronze Age farming settlement, probably a one-family concern. This is the enclosure and hut circle we have just examined. The immense double wall further down the hill is thought to be the result of a later attempt to fortify the site, probably by the people of the late Bronze Age or early Iron Age, at a time, perhaps round about 500 B.C., when fresh immigrants from the Continent were arriving in

Britain and attempting to dispossess those already here.

We have now arrived at the summit of Dewerstone Hill which we find to consist of a rather insignificant low tor. Here it is quite obvious that the stone mason has been at work and several very large pieces of granite have been removed from the tor itself. There are also a number of inscriptions carved upon the rocks, including one which reads:

CARRINGTON

OBIT

II SEPTEMBRIS

MDCCCXXX

Nicholas Carrington, the Dartmoor poet who died in 1830, seems to have been very fond of this spot and lingered here often.

From the top of Dewerstone Tor our field of vision has been greatly extended and from here we can see the distant hills of Bodmin Moor away to the west. If we walk SE along the rocky top of the tor we shall come to a spot where there is a sheer drop below us of 200 feet or more. Immediately below the Dewerstone, as this great mass of rock is called, is a densely wooded gorge, the trees being nearly all oaks. At all times of the year the roar of the river can be heard below but when the leaves are on the trees it cannot be seen. In winter and early spring however, glimpses of the Plym, foaming over the boulders that lie in its bed, can be caught from the top of the rock. There is a very steep, rocky and even dangerous path which leads from the top of the rock to the river below. This has been so eroded by constant use in recent years that the owners of the land, the National Trust, have asked that walkers do not use it but find an alternative route. This we will do now, and a very interesting route it will prove to be.

Before leaving the Dewerstone, however, we must just mention its place in local folk-lore. As those familiar with Dartmoor legends will know, Dewer was the Demon Huntsman of the Moor. Dewer was of course the Devil and his main sport seems to have been hunting the souls of unbaptised babies over the Moor. He had other quarries too apparently, erring adults among them. These his Yeth hounds – coal black with flaming eyes – used to pursue across Dartmoor, always eventually arriving at the Dewerstone. Here, with the victim in full flight and the hounds in full cry, the quarry was driven over the edge of the cliff on to the rocks below. As this happened the Demon Huntsman and his hounds would disappear leaving the lifeless victim below. There is a story that on one occasion, after a fall of snow, the imprint of a single naked human foot was found in the snow on the summit of the Dewerstone. Nearby were the footprints of dogs and also of cloven hooves. Obviously the Devil was hunting on foot on this occasion.

We now proceed to the western end of the summit and then walk westward and downward through the oakwoods. Very soon we shall strike a path into which we turn right-handed. This takes us past a couple of small quarries and close to a place where the quarrymen used to dispose of their waste rock by tipping it down the hillside below. The path is quite wide and slopes gently downward and was clearly at one time a tramway leading from the quarry. Here and there along the track are large dressed stones, abandoned after being worked on. Did they fall off the trucks perhaps?

Soon we see through the trees and below us to the left a broad sloping track with stone sleepers laid at intervals along it and then ahead of us a ruined building. The building housed the winding gear which winched the trucks up and down the inclined plane that we saw through the trees. The sequence of operations seems to have been as follows. The granite was quarried near the Dewerstone and having been dressed was loaded on to trucks. These were drawn by horses up and down the tramway along which we have just walked. On arrival at the junction of the tramway and the inclined plane which carried two parallel lines of rails, the trucks were manoeuvred onto one of the latter and attached to a cable which was wound around one of the two drums of the winding gear. The other drum also had a cable which was extended down the inclined plane and attached to the empty trucks waiting below. At a given signal the loaded trucks were started off down the incline, the drum turning as the cable paid out. As this happened the other cable wound on to its drum and the empty trucks were drawn up the incline by the weight of the laden ones going down. The laden trucks eventually found their way along a system of tracks which connected with the South Devon Railway near Goodameavy, about half a mile away. The Dewerstone quarries went out of business about a hundred years ago but the remains of the winding gear can still be found in the ruined building mentioned earlier, together with the great steel axle upon which the drums revolved.

We now turn to the SW and follow the inclined plane downward, taking care not to slip as we cross the granite sleepers. Two hundred yards or so further on, by which time the plane has deteriorated into a rubbly track, we merge with another track coming up from the right. We go ahead, as the track curves to the left, and then come onto a meticulously "crazy-paved" track, which zig-zags down the hillside to the river below. On reaching the stream – this is the Plym again – we turn downstream and soon come to Shaugh Bridge where the Plym is joined by the Meavy. This is a place with splendid river scenery and a good place for a picnic. It is a resort for hundreds of people who come out at weekends from Plymouth and other places nearby. The woods here are owned by the National Trust. It will be noticed that there are traces of ruined buildings on both sides of the river here. There is said to have been a paper mill north of the river in the late 18th and early 19th century. On the further side the ruins are those of buildings connected with the china clay industry.

To get to the further side of the Plym we use the wooden footbridge which spans the river just upstream from Shaugh Bridge itself. The latter carries the road which, having come up from the south by way of Shaugh Prior village, makes its way by a devious route to places on the western borders of Dartmoor, such as Hoo Meavy, Meavy, Clearbrook and Yelverton, all places to be visited on some future occasion.

Having crossed to the south side of the river we walk along the road for a few yards where we find a small parking place on the left of the road. At the far side of the car park we see a flight of steps leading to the top of a high bank. We can climb the steps and follow a path to the right, or we can follow the road for a few more yards. In either case we shall come to a path on the left with a signpost directing us to Cadover Bridge. This path runs more or less east to start with and winds its way among the trees which are growing among the spoil deposited here in the past from the now disused clay works. We are gradually gaining height and after about half a mile come out on to the edge of West Down and see one or two houses ahead.

We go left of the houses, either by way of the narrow path just inside the woods or by a hard track which comes up from the SW. If we do the latter we shall come to a gate where we rejoin the path. The path is now following the line, indeed it sometimes actually lies on top, of a pipeline constructed to bring china clay mixed with water from the clay pits near Cadover Bridge to the processing works that we saw a little while ago. This went on from 1880 until the 1960s. Now the pipeline is disused but still lies beneath our feet to be caught sight of every now and again as we proceed.

Soon the path emerges from the woods and runs in a north-easterly direction across West Down, just skirting the edge of the trees along a ledge halfway down the hillside. Below us we have the Plym again but we seldom see the water, so deep is the valley, but we can frequently hear it. As the path veers to the NE the Dewerstone comes into view and when we come abreast of it we realise what a tremendous rockpile it is. At one point the river turns almost at right-angles from SSW to NW and when we are just beyond this point we have the most magnificent view of all. Here we see, level with us on the opposite side of the gorge, the three great buttresses of the Dewerstone standing clear of the mantling of oaks which clothes the ravine. These buttresses are sheer above the river and well over 100 feet high. Above them are the rocks of Dewerstone Tor and on either side the oakwoods through which we came on our outward journey. To my mind the Dewerstone, seen from south of the river is one of the most noble sights in Devon. Whether I prefer it when the leaves are on the trees or when they are bare I have not yet made up my mind – I must go and have another look!

A few hundred yards further on we reach a gate through which the path goes to enter the North Wood. We are still on the pipe track with the river on our left and below us and so continue for about half a mile. Close to a farm called Dunstone we cross a little stream and directly ahead, over a steep little rise, we climb a short ladder, set against a wall. The path continues alongside the river for another quarter of a mile or so and then comes out onto a flat grassy area quite close to Cadover Bridge from which we started.

EXPLORATION 15. Dartmeet, Huccaby Cott, Huccaby Tor, Laughter Tor, Bellever Bridge, Snaily House, Babeny.

(CLEAR OF ALL FIRING AREAS)

Starting place:
Dartmeet, between Ashburton and Two Bridges. Map reference 671731.

Approach:
From Plymouth, Tavistock, Okehampton, etc. to Two Bridges then via B3357. From Exeter, Torquay, Totnes, etc. by way of A38 to Ashburton, turning off at Peartree Cross.

Amenities:
All amenities at Ashburton. Cafe, etc. (Badgers Holt) at Dartmeet. Inn (Tavistock Inn) and shop and Post Office at Poundsgate, 2 miles east of starting place. Toilets at New Bridge, en route from Ashburton.

Parking for the exploration:
Ample off-road parking space at starting place.

Type of excursion:
Easy moorland walking, some tracks through plantations and along river. About 7 miles.

This excursion begins at Dartmeet, a most beautiful spot which just has to be visited by any newcomer to Dartmoor. Dartmeet stands at the foot of an extremely steep hill close to the spot where the East and West Dart rivers meet and where the road which links Ashburton with Tavistock crosses the East Dart just before that stream meets its sister. It is clear that this tiny settlement has had a local importance for centuries, for just up-stream from the present road bridge stand the remains of a much older bridge, a clapper in fact, which is now unfortunately in a ruinous condition. Long before the present road was engineered in the late 18th century the old track linking the Stannary Towns of Ashburton and Tavistock came this way. Probably because of the importance of the place as a river crossing a few humble dwellings sprang up and there is a record of a village school having been established here in the 19th century. To it no doubt came the children from the scattered moorland farms in the vicinity. Dartmeet itself lies in the parish of Widecombe-in-the-Moor, but once across the bridge going west we shall be in the Forest of Dartmoor.

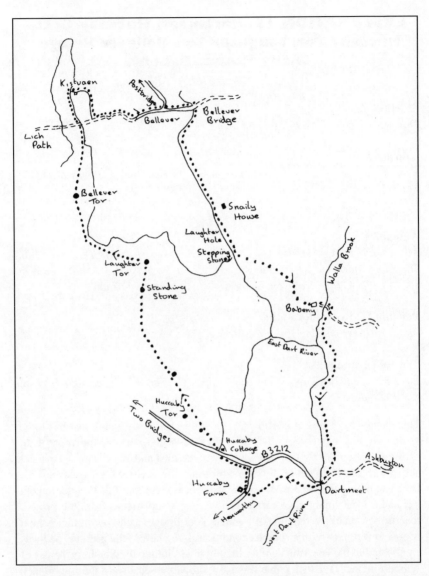

Having admired the splendid river scenery, we begin our expedition by crossing the bridge. Here the road swerves away to the right, going steeply uphill along a narrow stretch of road called Hart Hole Lane, no doubt a relic of the days when deer were found upon the Moor. Just beyond the bridge however we leave the road and make our way to the left, round the back of a house and petrol pumps, where we find a gate. Close to the gate is a signpost which indicates that beyond the gate lies a path linking Dartmeet with Huccaby. This path runs in a north-westerly direction across the rising ground for about 300 yards and then turns right into a narrow rocky lane which continues in the same direction for a similar distance. We cross a stile and emerge from the lane at a gate where we turn left.

We follow the path, marked by yellow-tipped posts, our course being about SW. Soon we reach a gate which brings us out on to the road opposite Huccaby Farm, where we turn right to a T-junction called Hexworthy Cross. Here we turn left and follow the road going NW which is now running parallel with a large plantation on our right. About 300 yards further on we come to the end of the wood. Here there is a cottage, called Huccaby Cott. Just beyond the cottage is a gate and passing through this we are within one of the great enclosures made in the 18th/19th centuries, which on Dartmoor are called newtakes.

Inside the gate two paths will be found, one going off to the north, the other to the NW. The first of these goes by way of Bellever to Postbridge, the second, the one we are going to take, also goes to Bellever and also to Bellever Tor. As we proceed the ground rises and soon we are passing Huccaby Ring, a prehistoric enclosure, and then the low rocks of Huccaby Tor. From this vantage point fine views are obtained to the north, NW and south. Our path continues NW for some distance, over fairly level ground and soon we pass Outer Huccaby Ring, another enclosure and then ahead of us we see a wall and a track running NE/SW. This is the Postman's Road – and that is literally what it used to be.

This old track was the route used by the local postman on his daily round on horseback, delivering letters to the scattered and isolated farms and villages in the vicinity of Princetown and Postbridge. This method of delivery went on until well after the last war and many were the hair-raising adventures experienced by the dedicated postman on his winter rounds.

In this immediate vicinity will be found also several deep gullies and shafts connected with the old Brimpts Tin Mine. On the further side of the wall a low pile of rock will be seen a little way to the north. This is Laughter Tor – more properly Lough Tor – and in front of it we see two objects.

The first of these is a fine standing stone whose name is Laughter Man. This stands at the head of a badly robbed double stone row, many of whose stones have obviously gone into the stone wall which bisects it. Laughter Man stands about 8 feet high and was restored to its proper

Laughter Man

position many years ago by the Dartmoor Exploration Committee of the Devonshire Association, the stone having fallen many years before that.

The second object referred to stands between Laughter Man and the tor. This is a large rectangular enclosure with high walls. It is built of granite and at first glance gives the impression of a ruined building which has lost its roof. Consideration however brings one to the conclusion that this cannot have been a building as the span of the roof would have been too great to be practicable without internal support, of which there is no sign. Local folk-lore, again quoted by Crossing, refers to this enclosure as the Sheep Measure. As one local resident said to me, "You know how many sheep it will hold so you drives 'em into it until it's full, then you know how many you have." Simpler but less accurate than the pocket calculators used by so many people these days?

From the Sheep Measure we make for Laughter Tor which is a low pile of scattered rocks with masses of bilberries (whortleberries) growing all around. From the tor, looking to the NW over the tops of the trees in the Bellever plantations, we can see the grey head of Bellever Tor about three-quarters of a mile away and to this we now make our way, skirting the edge of the forest as we go. There is a wall between the two tors but a convenient gateway gives us access and soon we are mounting the grassy sides of what is certainly one of Dartmoor's most famous tors.

This high scattered pile occupies a position at the southern end of a wide corridor which almost but not quite severs the eastern half of the Bellever plantations from that on the west. These plantations however have been here for less than 70 years. For many years, before that, possibly for centuries, the tor occupied an important place in local communal activities. Here in former days a great annual picnic used to take place on a specified Friday in April when the Dart Vale Harriers used to meet on the tor. Dartmoor folk from miles around attended these gatherings which were regarded as the highlight of the year's activities. These events seem not to have been held since the First World War.

Bellever Tor stands at 1456 feet above sea-level, which does not place it among the highest on the Moor. It is certainly among the most spectacular however because of its shapely lines and the beauty of its rock formations. Here the granite appears to have been built up in layers and the weathering that has taken place during the millions of years that have elapsed since its creation has worn away the softer rock thus emphasising the layers and leaving a ribbed effect which is both beautiful and striking.

As has been said, Bellever Tor is almost but not quite surrounded by Forestry Commission plantations. It stands in fact at the southern end of a wide corridor running south to north and well over a mile in length. This corridor,

Bellever Bridge

which varies in width from about 150 yards at the northern end to getting on for half a mile at the southern end, is enclosed by a belt of trees on the north and a stone wall to the south. The whole area, including the tor itself, formerly comprised part of the farm lands belonging to Bellever Farm, one of the Ancient Tenements of the Forest. These ancient farms, several of which still exist, were founded in medieval times and mostly lie in the vicinity of Postbridge, Dartmeet and Hexworthy.

It is said that one particular farmer who held Bellever in the late 19th century devoted most of his life to clearing the area now covered by Bellever Forest (Lakehead Hill is its local name). This consisted of removing as much of the surface rock as possible to make cultivation practicable and it is said that in the process he destroyed hundreds of hut-circles, kistvaens and other prehistoric remains. He left some however, as we shall see as we proceed.

From the summit of the tor we descend in a north-easterly direction to the edge of the plantations and then walk northwards along the edge. A little over a quarter of a mile will bring us to a spot where a wide well-marked track emerges from the forest on the right, crosses the corridor and enters the forest on the further side. This is the Lich Path or the Path of the Dead, along which it is said, in the early days of the Ancient Tenements, the dead were taken for burial in the churchyard at Lydford. In 1260 the Bishop of Exeter gave permission for some of the residents in the Forest to go to Widecombe Church, instead of Lydford, but there is no doubt that this route was much used long after that date.

A couple of hundred yards beyond this track a yellow tipped pole will be seen sticking out of the ground. This marks the site of a kistvaen or prehistoric burial place and there is another, this time surrounded by a circle of stones, about two hundred yards further on. Nearby, on the edge of the plantations to the west, another will be found in a little clearing among the trees. Right at the far end of the corridor will be found what is called an enclosed hut settlement, in other words a walled compound in which stood a number of Bronze Age dwellings; there is a single hut-circle just to the south and outside the compound. Unfortunately, the enclosed settlement has been badly robbed, probably by the farmer mentioned earlier and for this reason it is not a good specimen.

If for any reason we do not wish to examine the whole catalogue of remains in the vicinity it may be a good idea to select one good one and be content with that. In this case, having reached the Lich Path we cross it and continue north along the edge of the plantations for about 400 yards when, over the brow of the hill, we shall come to a spot where there is a small clearing among the trees just inside the forest.

In this clearing stands one of the finest kistvaens in the whole of Dartmoor. It consists of a stone chest, made of slabs of granite and quite large enough to accommodate the body of an adult. It stands well above the ground and is partially surrounded by the remains of a circle of standing stones. Going off roughly eastward are a number of stones which seem to be part of a stone row, but this row stops dead and it may not be what it seems. This splendid monument was restored by the Devonshire Association many years ago and that great authority on Dartmoor, Richard Hansford Worth, later expressed some doubt about the authenticity of the restoration. Even so, it is a most impressive relic.

From the clearing in which stands the kistvaen we have just examined, a path runs through the trees to the east and soon emerges upon a forest track. Here we turn right and continue for some distance until we reach a cross-roads where we turn left. This soon brings us to the edge of the fields above Bellever Youth Hostel, and following the track as it turns first right and then left we pass the hostel on our left and emerge upon the road near Bellever Bridge. This is a very pleasant spot, noted for the beauty of the stream – the East Dart – and the old and ruined clapper bridge just downstream from the more modern road bridge. That this is an ancient crossing place there can be no doubt, probably dating from the 13th century when the first farms were founded in the area. The road upon which we are now standing connects the farms in the vicinity of Cator and Widecombe with Postbridge and in part at least was probably formed along the old Lich Path.

Before we leave this place we must of course examine the clapper bridge. This we shall find is built of massive slabs of granite upon piers of the same stone. Unfortunately however, the bridge lacks its centre span. Indeed there is some doubt about this point. William Crossing in his *Guide to Dartmoor* refers to the fact that the centre span is missing and says that he found out who it was who tipped the great stone into the river. But no such stone is to be seen in the river bed though it is of course conceivable that it has since been removed from where it fell. However, some years ago it was pointed out that on either side of where the missing stone would have rested notches have been cut which may well have accommodated the timbers of a wooden centre section, though whether this was instead of or in substitution for a centre stone no-one can tell. The mystery seems likely to remain unanswered.

Having examined the bridge we cross to the further

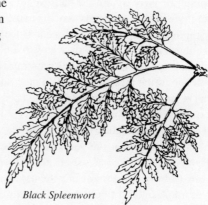

Black Spleenwort

(eastern) side and take the path which runs downstream alongside the river. We have high, rising ground on our left, and after about three-quarters of a mile we pass through a gap in a wall and enter a cleared forestry plantation area. (There has been extensive clearance of conifers on both sides of the river here.) We soon see, up on the hillside, the ruins of two fair sized buildings. This is the site of a farm, the higher building always these days called Snaily House but whose proper name was White's Slade. The other building was a barn.

This place is associated with one of those strange Dartmoor stories for the truth of which no-one can vouch but which may nevertheless have some truth in them. This one goes as follows. Long ago (as usual) two spinster sisters lived at White's Slade. They were the subject of much curiosity and speculation among their few neighbours because although they never seemed to work and kept no animals and had no visible means of subsistence, they were always plump and well fed. At last curiosity got the better of the neighbours and on an occasion when the sisters were away from home they broke into the house in an attempt to discover their secret. They did so, for although no ordinary provisions were found several large jars were discovered in which were quantities of black slugs, the sisters' sole item of diet. Some versions say that on their secret being discovered the sisters were so mortified that they pined away and died. Another account has it that they moved away and that one of them died soon after but that the other survived her by some years. Whatever the truth may be it seems certain that Snaily House has not been occupied since.

We now continue along the river bank for about 500 yards when we see, on the further side of the stream, a substantial house. This is Laughter Hole House and here a bridlepath comes down to the stream on the western side and crosses the river to join the path we are on. There are stepping stones here too and if we wished we could cross the river and make our way back to Dartmeet by rejoining our original path near Huccaby Cottage. This would not materially shorten our walk however and so, unless there is some good reason to the contrary, we continue without crossing the river. At the stepping stones our path leaves the river by way of a gate and goes up over the hill, with a field wall to our right. Soon we leave the open moorland and enter a stroll or wide corridor between walls. The land rises at first but soon begins to fall and, after passing through a gate, brings us into the farmyard of a farm called Babeny.

This is another of the Ancient Tenements of the Forest; it was certainly in existence as early as 1260 because the people who lived here were among those licensed by the Bishop to use Widecombe Parish Church instead of Lydford. A mill was built here about 1302, the King providing the timber, the rest of the cost falling upon the tenants of the Forest. We leave the farmyard by a gateway on the eastern side and cross a little bridge spanning a stream. The stream is the Walla Brook and by crossing it we have left the Forest and are now in Widecombe parish.

Having crossed we turn right and follow the stream downstream passing as we go a small and beautiful clapper bridge of three openings. Soon we come to the spot where the Walla Brook falls into the East Dart, which by now has become quite a considerable stream. We are now at the foot of high rising ground to the south and south-east. This is Yartor Down and on its summit, more than 500 feet above us, are the rocks of Yar Tor itself. This valley has been described by a famous Dartmoor lover – the Rev. Sabine Baring-Gould – as one of the most beautiful spots on the Moor. Our path now lies along the line of the river. The going is somewhat rough and in a wet season decidedly splashy, but not impassable.

About half a mile beyond the confluence of the East Dart and the Walla Brook a ruined building with one gable end standing will be seen among the trees on the further side of the river. This is Dolly's Cot about which a strange story is told. It is said that nearly two hundred years ago a local man, morose and saturnine by nature, married a beautiful and attractive girl. Apparently the girl

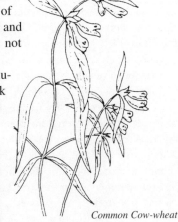

Common Cow-wheat

124

was much admired by men other than her husband and to remove her from temptation he built this lonely cottage and installed his bride in it. It seems that in later years a rumour was circulated that one of the men whose attentions to Dolly was resented by her husband was the then Prince of Wales who later became Prince Regent and later still King George IV. There seems to be no basis of truth in this story, the only connection being that the Prince was of course Duke of Cornwall and consequently owner of the land upon which the cottage stood.

Half a mile further on the ground becomes less rough and then ahead of us we see the buildings at Badgers Holt and Dartmeet. If we take the left-hand path when the track forks this will bring us directly to the car park. The right-hand path takes the weary explorer to the cafe and a well earned cup of tea and/or other refreshment.

EXPLORATION 16. Trendlebere Down, Houndtor Wood, Lustleigh Cleave, Hisley Wood.

(CLEAR OF ALL FIRING AREAS)

Starting place:
Trendlebere Down near Bovey Tracey. Map reference 782793.

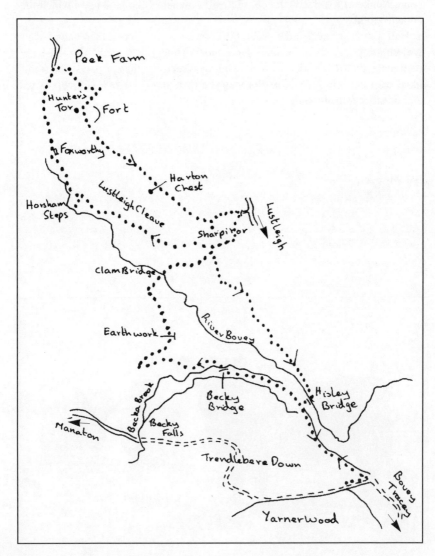

Approach:

From Exeter, Torquay, Plymouth, etc. by way of Bovey Tracey then towards Manaton 2½ miles.

From Tavistock via B3212 by way of Two Bridges as far as Watching Place Cross then turning right through Manaton.

From Moretonhampstead by way of B3212 then turning left at Watching Place Cross through Manaton. (Watching Place Cross is approximately 7 miles from the starting place.)

Amenities:

All amenities at Bovey Tracey. Public house (Kestor Inn), Post Office and shop at Manaton, 2 miles from starting place. Public house (Cleave Hotel), Post Office and shop and toilets at Lustleigh.

Parking for the exploration:

Ample off-road parking in vicinity of starting place, especially south of road.

Type of excursion:

Good going, mostly along tracks and paths. There are a few steep gradients but none of any great length. In summer the bracken along the paths in Lustleigh Cleave is very tall and dense. For this reason the Cleave should be avoided immediately following heavy rain as in these circumstances a wetting is almost unavoidable. About 7 miles.

Black Galloway and Highland cattle

Trendlebere Down, the starting place for this excursion, is in my opinion one of the most beautiful valleys in Devon. Here the land sweeps down, precipitously in places, from the high ground of Haytor Down and Black Hill to the valley of the River Bovey, falling over a thousand feet in little over a mile. Having parked we walk back eastward along the road for a few yards, until we come to the edge of a plantation on our left. Here a rough road will be found going off to the left (NW) and descending the very steep hillside. This is the old Manaton Road, along which all traffic from Bovey Tracey to Manaton used to go until the modern road which we have just left was engineered in the 19th century. It seems likely that very few vehicles ever used this road and the traffic would have consisted almost exclusively of pedestrians, horsemen and pack-horses. After a few hundred yards the land flattens out somewhat and soon we find that we are on the floor of the valley. All the time we have been drawing nearer to the river – the Bovey – and now we come to a short lane on our right which leads to the stream which is here spanned by a lovely little hump-backed bridge, a pack-horse bridge in fact. This is Hisley Bridge. It stands in Hisley Wood and we shall see it again towards the end of our excursion.

Hisley Bridge

Meanwhile, we go back to the old Manaton Road and continue along it through the woods, passing another side-track which goes over a wooden bridge. As we proceed we shall see that the river on our right is getting further away from us but soon we come to another bridge, spanning a bustling little stream – the Becky Brook – which comes steeply down the hillside from the west having fallen over the famous Becky Falls which lie about a mile or so upstream from us. Having crossed Becky Bridge we continue for a few hundred yards until we come to a spot where the old road continues to the NW but a branch swings round away to the right. We follow the latter for about half a mile as it goes up the hillside. When we come to a point where our track is crossed by another we turn right. Soon we take a narrow path which forks left, marked by an arrow painted on a tree. As we approach the top of the hill, along the edge of Houndtor Wood, the site of an Iron Age earthwork lies to our right. This is one of many fortifications built above the river valleys around Dartmoor by the people who lived in these parts between 500 and 200 B.C. as a defensive measure when they were threatened by immigrants from Western Europe. Our path goes steeply downhill and meets another at right-angles. Here we turn right, and soon reach the river at a point where it is crossed by a clam (wooden footbridge), which we cross.

Having crossed the bridge we are in Lustleigh Cleave. This is one of Devon's most famous and lovely valleys. The word cleave indicates a deep valley with rocky cliff-like sides and there are several such valleys around the Moor to which the name is applied. Lustleigh Cleave is something less than two miles in length and through it, from NW to SE, flows the River Bovey. The land on the north-eastern side of the cleave is largely open, rocky common land, sloping steeply down to the river. On the south-western side the valley is densely wooded.

From the footbridge our path takes us up the steep hillside to the NE for about 500 yards. During this climb we shall pass two paths which come in from the right. At each of these points our path goes uphill to the left, and a short distance beyond the second junction we turn left at a post indicating Foxworthy Bridge. We walk along the hillside for nearly a mile, losing height steadily as we go. As we get lower the land flattens out and we see that we are again only a couple of hundred yards from the river. We now reach a side-path going off to the left and following this we are soon on the river bank. We reach the stream at a place called Horsham Steps.

These are no ordinary stepping stones however, although the path does cross the river here. At some time in the distant past a collection of enormous boulders have been washed down the river and have jammed at this spot with the result that, except at times when the river is in full spate, it disappears altogether below the rocks, reappearing again a little lower down.

This is a wonderful place to visit in winter when the tumbled rocks, the rushing water, the overhanging trees and the general air of grandeur combine to present a spectacle not easily equalled, even in beautiful Devon. If we crossed the river at Horsham Steps a walk of less than a mile would bring us to Manaton Church, but this is a visit we must defer for the time being. Instead we return to the path we left a short time ago and on reaching it we turn left.

A walk of about a quarter of a mile will bring us to Foxworthy Farm and Mill. Here there is an ancient and beautiful farmhouse, lovingly restored; at the mill the water wheel is still in position. Beyond the farm we enter a narrow green lane which runs northward and after about half a mile emerges on the road where we turn right to a farm called Peck. Beside the farm a gate gives access to a field through which the path runs uphill back to Lustleigh Cleave, which we gain via another gate. We continue to climb for a little while, and turning right at a wall, soon find ourselves on the more or less flat top of a ridge with the deep valley of the cleave on our right. Ahead of us are the rocks of Hunter's Tor and going through a gate nearby we come to the scanty remains of an earthwork and enclosure referred to on the map as a "fort". This is another of the Iron Age fortifications referred to earlier.

Scotch Blackface

The vicinity of Hunter's Tor is the scene of one of Dartmoor's lesser known "hauntings". Unusually this one happens in broad daylight. It seems that the startled observer sees a party of horsemen riding towards him along the ridge. Nothing very unusual about this you may think. But these horsemen are gorgeously dressed in the rich hunting attire of the 14th/15th century. They are riding splendidly caparisoned horses; they have hawks upon their wrists and are accompanied by hunt servants on foot and hunting dogs. Suddenly the whole party, riders, horses, hawks, servants and dogs disappear as though they had never been. You don't believe it? Well perhaps not, but Dartmoor is a strange place and strange things happen here.

Our route now lies for a mile or more along the top of the ridge, and as tree cover increases we go past the great rock called Harton Chest to another group of rocks – Sharpitor. According to the map there is a logan stone (a rocking stone) called Nutcrackers here, but alas it has gone. According to the local story the Nutcracker rock was displaced in the early 1950s by vandals. It is said that an attempt was made by an Army group stationed locally to replace the stone on its seating. To do this they raised the stone in a sling made of steel rope by means of sheer-legs. Unfortunately the stone slipped from its sling and fell down the side of the Cleave to a position from which it could not be recovered. You will have to crack your nuts elsewhere I fear!

From Sharpitor we continue steeply downhill, ignoring a side-path to our left, and come to a gate. We don't go through the gate, but take a path which goes steeply uphill to the right. As it levels out and begins to descend we come to a spot known locally as Heaven's Gate, from which the splendid views once seen are now obscured by young broad-leaved trees. Nearby on the right are several Bronze Age hut circles.

We pass a path going off the right (which we took on our outward journey) and going ahead, retrace our steps a little way, taking the next path to the left. In about 500 yards the path again forks. Here we go down to the right and, crossing a stile, follow a path which runs for about half a mile.

A careful lookout will reveal two ruined buildings built into the hillside to the left of the track. One of these, the first we come to going SE, seems to have been a farm building. The building is very ruinous but there is a conduit which conveyed the water from the site under the track and then down the steep slope to the river below. There is also a sunken track approaching the site from Higher Hisley. The second building may have been a dwelling; the remains of the partitions between the rooms are still to be seen. Nothing seems to be known about the history of these buildings except the name, which was Bovey Combe, but in the woods all around there are many traces of ancient mining works and it is possible that the buildings were connected with these. About half-way along this path we shall find that our track is running along a kind of shelf cut out of the hillside above the river.

We are now about a quarter of a mile from the river at the pack-horse bridge in Hisley Wood which we saw earlier in the day. At this beautiful spot we may well stop and rest. Indeed if the time of year is right – late spring – a short excursion downstream before crossing will be rewarded by the sight of a veritable sea of bluebells. However, eventually we have to cross the bridge and then on the further side we find the old Manaton Road down which we came at the outset of the expedition. We now turn left to face a stiffish climb up the side of Trendlebere Down but, if we take it steadily and with frequent stops, we soon reach the top a few yards from the spot where our cars are parked.

Thoughtful people reading the details of this exploration may have been struck by the fact that although Lustleigh Cleave is the area explored, the village of Lustleigh has not featured at all. The fact is of course that there are several different approaches to the Cleave and we have used only one of them.

It will be noticed as the exploration progresses that there are numerous guide-posts at the intersections of the various paths around the Cleave and it would be very easy for more ambitious explorers to devise their own routes. I heartily recommend this course of action; it can be most satisfying.

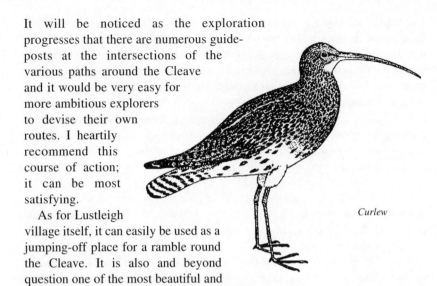

Curlew

As for Lustleigh village itself, it can easily be used as a jumping-off place for a ramble round the Cleave. It is also and beyond question one of the most beautiful and romantically sited villages in Devon. The combination here of ancient and beautiful church, village green, thatched houses, tiny stream (the River Wrey) and steep and narrow streets and an undulating landscape all go to make up a story-book village. Also the village has a number of unusual features. For example, the churchyard occupies a more or less circular site and is raised above the level of the surrounding area. This, together with the presence in the church of an inscribed stone of the pre-Saxon Christian period, has led some authorities to conjecture that, although the church is probably 13th to 15th century in date, nevertheless a church has existed here since the 6th century.* If this were true then Lustleigh would be among the earliest Christian sites in Devon.

Another feature of the village is its recreation ground or park – here it is called Town Orchard, for good reason as it has many apple trees which bear prolifically. In the orchard will be found the May Queen's chair where the

---

* For information about the significance of a church occupying a circular raised site and the presence of ancient inscribed stones in such churches see *The Kingdom of Dumnonia* by Susan M. Pearce, published by Lodenek Press, 1978.

The inscription on the stone at Lustleigh has been read as DATUIDOCI CONHINOCI FILIUS which is translated as DATUIDOC SON OF CONHINOC. The stone was probably a memorial to a British Christian named Datuidoc, no doubt a prominent person in his own time but about whom nothing is known at present.

chosen maiden is crowned annually on May Day. The chair is made of granite and is raised on an enormous granite boulder. The names of the past May Queens going back many years are inscribed on the boulder. The crowning ceremony was revived about 1919, after many years of neglect, by Cecil Torr, Lord of the Manor of Wreyland, whose venerable and beautiful thatched Manor House can be found on the banks of the Wrey about 200 yards from the village. Yes, Lustleigh has it all, including a splendid old pub (the Cleave Hotel) and a tea-shop where the traditional Devonshire cream tea can be found in its natural habitat.

EXPLORATION 17. Fernworthy Forest, Teignhead Farm, Newtake, Watern Tor, Watern Combe, Walla Brook, Shovel Down, Thornworthy Down.

(PARTLY WITHIN THE OKEHAMPTON FIRING AREA)

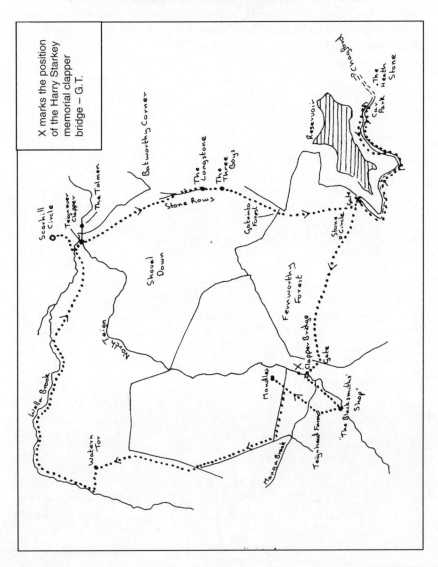

X marks the position of the Harry Starkey memorial clapper bridge – G.T.

Starting place:
Fernworthy Forest. Map reference 659838.

Approach:
By way of Chagford from all directions. Leave Chagford by the road which runs NW from the market square and fork left after about 100 yards. From here onwards follow signposts marked Fernworthy through narrow lanes for about 4 miles. After 4 miles Fernworthy reservoir and forest will be seen ahead and to the right. The road we are following enters the forest, when after a short distance the entrance to a car park will be seen on the right.

Amenities:
All amenities at Chagford. Toilets at Fernworthy car park.

Parking for the expedition:
In the main car park.

Type of excursion:
This is a typical Dartmoor walk which the experienced walker will take in his stride. There are some considerable gradients and a bit of rough country, but nothing that need disturb healthy people of all ages. About 12 miles the round trip.

N.B. The western extremity of this expedition coincides with the boundary of the Okehampton artillery range. It would be better not to attempt this walk on a firing day (see Introduction). Neither should the walk be attempted in bad weather or if mist is seen hovering over the Moor unless an experienced guide is available.

Fernworthy
stone cirle

The first part of our walk is way-marked by colour-coded posts; our route is the blue one. We leave the car park near the toilets and immediately turn left and then right on to the "Anglers road". We soon branch left and follow the way-markers between the trees, and then over a wooden footbridge into a grassy bird-watching area. We emerge on to the road that we left to drive into the car park, and here we turn right and follow the road to its end.

We pass through the hand-gate at the first gateway on the left, which gives access to the plantations to the west of the reservoir. This takes us along a wide forestry track which runs through the woods for well over a mile, climbing steadily all the way. The track forks a few hundred yards from the gate and here we take the left-hand track. About a third of a mile from the gate a grassy glade will be seen to the right of the track. If we diverge to the right here about 50 yards will take us to the Fernworthy stone circle. This is a sort of miniature Stonehenge about 64 feet in diameter. This monument is a relic of the prehistoric folk who lived upon Dartmoor, probably of the early Bronze Age, say 3800 years ago. There are about a dozen of these great stone circles on Dartmoor. Their exact purpose is not known but clearly they had some connection with the religious beliefs and practices of the people who erected them. Nearby also will be found the remains of two or three rows of standing stones which it is thought also had some place in the religious or funeral rites of the Bronze Age people. The Fernworthy rows are not very spectacular and as the stones are small they can easily be overlooked, surrounded as they are by trees.

Teignhead Bridge

Having examined the circle and stone rows we now return to the track and follow it more or less westward until we reach the edge of the plantations. Here we pass through a gate and find that we are looking westward across a fairly deep and wide valley in the bottom of which, only a couple of hundred yards away, flows a river. This is the North Teign, the more important half of the stream from which Teignmouth takes its name. We make our way down the somewhat rough grassy hillside to the river which here flows from left to right, that is from south to north. The track from the gate brings us to the river at a spot where the stream is spanned by a clapper bridge, that is, a bridge made by imposing slabs of granite upon piers built up of granite blocks without using mortar or any other binding agent.

This bridge, always referred to as the Teignhead Clapper, is apart from the one at Postbridge and perhaps one other, probably the finest of its kind to be found upon Dartmoor. However, although the Postbridge clapper and several others are thought to be medieval in origin this one has no such claim to antiquity. It was almost certainly built about the turn of the 18th/19th centuries and the marks of the drill used to split the slabs that form the roadway of the bridge testify to this. It is known that this method of splitting granite was not used upon Dartmoor much earlier than the beginning of the 19th century.

We cross the river at the bridge and make our way up stream, that is to the left, keeping as close to the river bank as we may. This may not be very close in places as the ground tends to be marshy, especially in a wet season. Having crossed a tiny tributary stream, the Manga Brook, and made our way through a variety of pits and gullies, we come back to the river at a point about 250 yards from the bridge. Here we find the tumbled and scanty ruins of an ancient building, right on the river bank, indeed the eastern wall overlooks the river itself.

This building is not marked on the map, not even the $2^1/_2$ inch sheet mentions it, but it has some very interesting features if carefully examined. For example, inside the building – it has no roof of course – is a great block of granite about $4^1/_2$ feet long by $2^1/_2$ feet high and about 21 inches wide. In the upper surface of this block are cut two very fine small troughs each a little over a foot long by about 9 inches wide and about 4 inches deep. The sides and ends

"The Blacksmith's Shop"
(N. Teign)
Block with two troughs

of these troughs are chamfered in a manner which is sometimes found in tinners' mould-stones in Dartmoor blowing-houses. This feature has led some people to suppose that the building we are now examining is a blowing-house itself. Personally, I do not think so,* because, although there are plenty of signs that the tinners have been active in the vicinity, there are no signs in this building of any wheel-pit to house the water-wheel, nor of a leat to bring water to the site nor of the furnace that was an essential part of the equipment of any blowing-house. Local people refer to this old building as "the blacksmith's shop" and when one remembers how much blacksmith's work there must have been associated with the old tinners – making, mending and sharpening tools for example – it seems not unlikely that this was the case. If this was so then the twin troughs we have seen were probably the blacksmith's quenching troughs and not mould-stones. However, a further careful search will bring to light a broken granite trough inside the house and a small complete one on top of the wall overlooking the river. These could well have been mould-stones, so perhaps the blacksmith was a stone-mason too and filled in his spare time by making mould-stones for use elsewhere.

On leaving the blacksmith's shop we mount the hill to the WNW and soon find that we are approaching the site of a ruined farm, with a small plantation of trees behind it. This is Teignhead farmhouse and its associated buildings, all now entirely ruinous. The farmhouse was built about 1808 to complement the great Teignhead enclosures which were taken in from the Forest at about that date. These enclosures, always referred to as the Teignhead Newtakes, extend over thousands of acres all around the farmhouse. The latter was last occupied as such before the last war; the newtakes are still rented by private graziers from the Duchy of Cornwall. From the farmhouse we walk NE along the hillside for about 400 yards until we come to a low granite wall which comes down the hill from our left. In this wall there is a gate and on passing through this we find ourselves in a narrow stroll, the walls of which converge as we progress northwards until we are in quite a narrow passage. The passage ends at a group of ruined buildings about 150 yards from the gate. On our left we see a long building, once clearly a single storey dwelling of three rooms. Behind this is an open courtyard and beyond and in line with the dwelling a large building which was probably a barn or something similar. Opposite the house is another building, also ruinous, of unknown purpose.

*Reconsideration of the site following the finding of a probable mortar stone near the building in 1938 has made me think that it may have been a blowing-house after all. It is now known that there are, in fact, signs of a leat, a wheel-pit and possibly a furnace.

This place is Mandles, sometimes called Manga by local people. It was the forerunner of Teignhead farmhouse and existed at a time when the enclosures here were much smaller. William Crossing refers to this place in his *Guide to Dartmoor* (though he puts it in the wrong place) and records that here one George Endacott, otherwise Teignhead George, brought up his numerous family. Mandles has not been occupied in living memory and perhaps not since the early years of the 19th century.

On leaving the abandoned farm we return to the gate at the end of the stroll and then make our way along the wall which runs WNW up the hill. We follow this wall, which eventually comes to an end, its line continuing as a low earthen bank. In about 700 yards from Mandles this boundary work meets another which goes NNW. We turn right along the latter, a bank-and-ditch arrangement, which in places is quite distinct and in others almost disappears, until after nearly three-quarters of a mile we come to a wall, which we cross by means of a ladder-stile. We now turn to the north and make our way towards the top of the ridge which lies to our left, gradually leaving the wall on our right. Here the ground is badly broken and strewn with loose boulders and some care is needed in traversing it.

Soon after leaving the wall we see ahead of us the rocks of Watern Tor, one of the great curiosities of this part of Dartmoor. No-one can claim that Watern Tor is one of the great tors of the Moor like Hound Tor or Great Mis Tor, but its scattered piles of rocks are spectacular in their own way. They are formed from thin layers of granite piled upon one another in such a way as to suggest an untidy pile of muffins. This has been caused by the weathering away of the softer rock between the layers and in places is very pronounced indeed. The northern pile of Watern Tor is always called the Thirlstone, a word meaning "the holed stone". Here there are two contiguous stacks of rock standing so close to one another and so shaped by the hand of nature as to have the appearance of an archway when seen from some angles. The Thirlstone is one of the bound-marks of the Forest and is mentioned in the

Teignever Bridge   *Wallabrook clapper*

original perambulation of 1240. When I last visited Watern Tor there was a Dartmoor post-box here, with the usual rubber stamp, visitors' book etc. The views from this spot are really quite splendid and on a fine day it is an ideal place for lunch. On a windy or showery day it would probably be more pleasant to find a suitable place lower down.

From Watern Tor we turn and walk due west down the steep hillside for about 350 yards. This brings us into a deep valley down which a moorland stream runs northward. This valley is Watern Combe and the stream is the Walla Brook. We turn and follow the stream northward, keeping our eyes well open as we go because in this valley, quite close to where we are now, are two ruined buildings, almost certainly tinners' shelters, which we may find if we look carefully. Both buildings are on the east side of the stream, one – the most likely for us to find – is at the northern end of the combe, above the bank of the stream.

Our course now lies along the stream which meanders wildly as it falls towards lower ground and eventually veers from north to east. In a wet season the ground along the stream tends to be marshy but not impassable. Generally speaking I have found that the best ground lies on the right bank but that changes of bank are desirable from time to time. Eventually, when we are about a mile from the spot where the river changed its course to east, we find that the ground is increasingly marshy and so we leave the stream and change our course to ESE. This soon brings us to higher and firmer ground where we turn to the east and make our way towards the point where the Walla Brook meets the North Teign. Here there are two clapper bridges, one across the Walla Brook and the other across the Teign. We are at the moment between the two streams. Before leaving this spot there are a couple of features that we ought to examine if we have time.

The first of these is the Tolmen. This is a great boulder which lies in the bed of the N. Teign just to the east of the clapper which spans that river. To reach it we cross the Walla Brook and then walk along the north bank of the N. Teign and find the Tolmen about 50 yards below the clapper. We now see that this great mass of rock is perforated from top to bottom by a round hole more than two feet in diameter. The beginnings of other holes can plainly be seen on the upper surface of the boulder. Although this is now known to be the work of nature there was a time, not so long ago, when magical properties were ascribed to this stone; local mothers whose children were suffering from whooping-cough used to bring them to the stone and pass them through the hole as this was thought to be beneficial to the suffering child. The name Tolmen means 'holed stone'.

On Gidleigh Common, about 300 yards north of the Tolmen, lies the

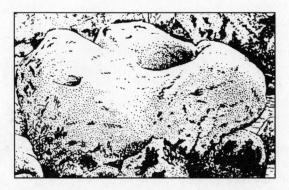

The holed stone in the Teign below Scorhill

Scorhill stone circle, one of the great prehistoric circles of Dartmoor. This one is about 90 feet in diameter and the stones of which it is composed are larger than any of the others on the Moor, the tallest being over 8 feet high. As previously stated these circles date from the early Bronze Age, perhaps 1800 BC or thereabouts.

From the circle we make our way back to the clapper over the Walla Brook; having crossed we make for the Teignever Clapper bridge over the N. Teign which we also cross. Depending upon the time of year we shall certainly be struck by the beauty of our surroundings. In early autumn when the rowan trees which fringe the river are changing colour but have not yet lost their leaves and still carry their harvest of scarlet berries, the scene is most spectacular. The combination of the rushing stream, the lichen covered boulders, the colour of the trees and the venerable bridge are almost breathtaking. The bridge, by the way, may or may not be ancient in itself, but the crossing place certainly is. It is said that as far back as medieval times the church path from the farms around Fernworthy to Gidleigh crossed the river at this spot.

Shovel Down

Having crossed the river we now make our way up the sloping ground to the SE. To our left we shall see a wall, but although we follow the line of this we keep well away from it as the ground near the wall tends to be very muddy. After a while the land flattens out and then begins to rise again. When we are about 1000 yards from the river we notice that the wall on our left has disappeared, having veered away to the north at a spot called Batworthy Corner. We continue our course up the hillside but change direction to almost due south.

Cuckoo

Soon we see ahead of us a number of stone pillars erect upon the common and these quickly resolve themselves into a complex of rows of stones. These are the famous Shovel Down antiquities. They consist of the remains of at least seven rows of stones, five of which were double rows; the longest surviving row is about 200 yards in length. The rows lie on either side of the ridge and involved with them are at least three burial places, one of which is surrounded by a fourfold circle of standing stones, a very unusual feature. It seems certain that these ancient monuments, also Bronze Age in date, were badly damaged by the activities of the wall-builders of an earlier age and it is also probable that there were formerly more burial sites than can now be seen.

The southernmost of these rows leads directly to the Longstone, a tall granite pillar which stands about 11 feet high. This great stone was clearly once part of the complex we have just seen, but centuries ago it was adopted as a boundary mark for the Forest of Dartmoor and the parishes of Gidleigh and Chagford, and in token of this status it bears the initials DC (Duchy of Cornwall), GP (Gidleigh Parish) and an oddly-shaped C (for Chagford).

The Longstone – Shovel Down

Standing at the Longstone and looking around, we see to the NE in the near distance Kestor Rock, which stands on the summit of the ridge about half a mile away. About the same distance to the ENE are the rocks of

Middle Tor and to the SE is Thornworthy Tor. The latter stands on Thornworthy Down, which is contained entirely within a walled enclosure. We continue southwards and come to another stone, less impressive and leaning, the last survivor of "The Three Boys", and from here we make our way down the slope to the SSW, to a gate in the forest fence, a short distance to the right of the Thornworthy enclosure wall.

Inside the gate there is a wide forest track which we follow, turning neither right nor left when it meets other tracks, until going down a slope we join a track which we soon recognise as one along which we came earlier. In a couple of hundred yards we come out on to the road, where we turn right and make our way back to the car park.

EXPLORATION 18. Zoar Common, Hill Bridge, Horndon Bridge, Cudlipptown, White Tor, Langstone Moor, Stooky Moor, Lynch Tor, Baggator Gate.

(PARTLY WITHIN THE MERRIVALE FIRING AREA)

Starting place:
Zoar, Mary Tavy. Map reference 523807.

Approach:
From all directions by Okehampton/Tavistock road – A386, turning off east at Mary Tavy into road signposted Horndon and Zoar.

Amenities:
All amenities at Tavistock and Okehampton. Toilets and Post Office/shop at Mary Tavy. Public house (Elephant's Nest) at Horndon, 1 mile SW of starting place.

Parking for the exploration:
Clear of road at starting place. There is ample space by the unmetalled road running north across the common from the hamlet of Zoar.

Type of excursion:
Some tracks and paths with a good deal of open moorland. Two or three moderate climbs of no great length. The going may be muddy and/or splashy in places. About 9 miles the round trip. Partly within the Merrivale firing area – check firing programme before starting.

Our starting place for this excursion is the ancient hamlet of Zoar, which lies within the parish of Mary Tavy. As will be seen, the area has been the subject of much activity on the part of the mining fraternity in years past. Copper, tin, lead, silver, zinc and arsenic have all been produced by local mines at various times.

Having parked we return to the road along which we came from Mary Tavy and turn left into it, i.e. to the NE. A short distance along we come to a metalled road going off to the right across an area of open common. This brings us to the gate of Lower Creason Farm. Here the road turns hard left and there is a finger post indicating a footpath. The road now becomes a rough track which we follow. It then becomes a lane running between walls and we

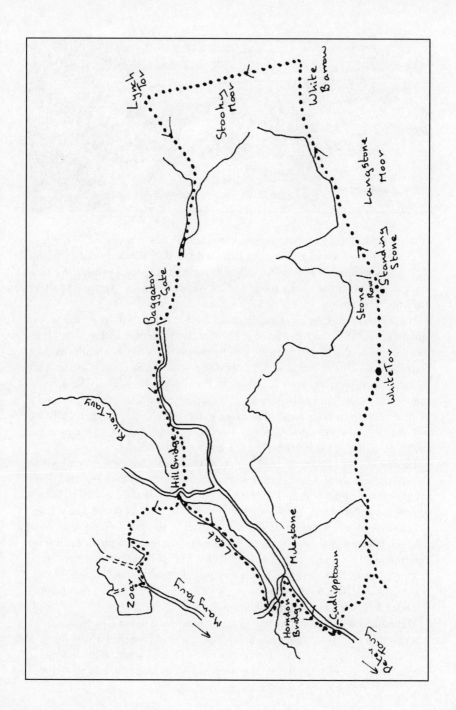

145

Hill Bridge

come to a gate through which we go. As the lane winds between fields it brings us first to Lower Town and then to Hill Bridge Farm. Beyond the latter farm there is a dwelling on the right which was formerly the local school. We now reach a gate with the road beyond. A few yards down the road is the River Tavy and Hill Bridge.

We leave Hill Bridge by climbing down an iron runged ladder on the down-stream side at the northern end of the bridge. Before doing so however let us have a look at the bridge itself. It will be noticed that this is a fairly modern construction. This is because the old bridge was washed away in the 19th century when the river rose in spate after a sudden downpour. The Tavy is notorious for this kind of behaviour; it is said to be capable of rising as much as nine feet in an hour or so. The oblong apertures in the parapet walls are intended to allow the flood water to flow through and so relieve the pressure on the structure of the bridge when the water rises suddenly.

Having climbed down the ladder we now find ourselves on the river bank at the spot where there is a weir and where a leat comes off the river and flows more or less parallel with it. The leat was constructed in the early 19th century to provide water power for a complex of mines in the vicinity of Mary Tavy. Wheal Friendship was one of these and from it tin, copper and lead were produced at various times. It will be noticed that the leat is maintained in good condition and still carries a full head of water. This is because the water is now employed to work a turbine which generates electricity which is fed into the National Grid. The broad shallow steps in the river bed are a "fish ladder" intended to assist the salmon in their migration.

Our path now lies along the leat so that we have the river on our left and the leat on our right. We continue along this path for about a mile, passing through Creason Wood as we go. Eventually we come to a spot where a lane intersects the leat and here we turn left into the steep and rocky lane which runs downhill

146

to the river. The river is spanned at this spot by Horndon Bridge and we cross to the further side, stopping a moment to appreciate the glorious river scenery both up and down stream.

On the further side of the bridge the lane rises steeply for two or three hundred yards and finally emerges upon a metalled road running right and left. This is the road which connects Peter Tavy with Mary Tavy via Hill Bridge. Note the stone guide post at the junction of the lanes, also serving as a milestone, another example of 18th/19th century frugality.

We now turn right as for Peter Tavy but only walk along the road for about six hundred yards until we come to a cluster of houses and a road going off to the left. We have reached Cudlipptown, one of the ancient sub-manors belonging to Tavistock Abbey. It seems to have come into the possession of the abbey in the late 11th or early 12th century and remained part of the abbey lands until the Dissolution. An interesting aspect of this association is that Cudlipptown remained part of the parish of Tavistock until the late 19th century, despite the fact that it was entirely detached from that town, being completely surrounded by the parishes of Peter Tavy and Mary Tavy.

At Cudlipptown we turn left into the lane which goes off to the east and follow this as it meanders between farms, houses and fields until it eventually emerges upon the open moor about three-quarters of a mile from the point at which we entered it. Our course along this lane should be nominally eastward, changing to NE when a house called Broadmoor is seen ahead. A branch going off to the south across a stream should be ignored. Once the common is reached – this is Cudlipptown Down – our course should be as nearly eastward as we can make it. We are now rising steadily but despite this the going is good and we should make good headway.

We are making for White Tor which lies ahead of us about half a mile away and which will soon be in full view. On the common all around are a variety of hut circles, enclosures and cairns, all relics of the prehistoric people who lived here more than two thousand years ago. When we reach the tor we shall find that it is a large scattered pile from which wide views can be obtained in almost every direction except to the north where the high ground of northern Dartmoor intervenes.

One item of interest should be noted. A search will show that at some time attempts have been made to throw a wall around the upper part of the tor incorporating some of the natural rock piles. It has been suggested that this was a defensive operation and that these fortifications were perhaps erected by the then residents at a time when they feared an attempt by fresh arrivals to dispossess them of their land and/or their belongings. It will be seen that there are a number of hut circles inside this wall.

From the summit of White Tor we make our way eastward, making for the track running WSW/ENE across the common. On our way we pass another despoiled cairn and then a good kistvaen. We reach the track close to a standing stone that has been in view for some time. This is the Langstone from which the part of the moor we are now on takes its name – Langstone Moor. This great menhir stands over 9 feet high and is the terminal stone of a stone row over 100 yards long. There is a burial place – a cairn – at the other end. Unfortunately the cairn has almost disappeared and only a dozen or so of the stones in the row still remain.

It will be noticed that the menhir presents a rather pockmarked appearance. This is because it was used as a target by machine gunners during the Second World War. About half a mile to the SE lies the Langstone Moor circle which was similarly badly treated by soldiers under training at that time. If we wish to visit this we can do so but it is not advisable to make a bee-line for it from the Langstone because of the marshy conditions of the ground. Instead we continue SE along the track which diverges here and follow this for about 600 yards when the circle will come into view away to the right.

The Langstone

If we do not wish to visit the circle we continue NE along the main track. Soon we shall find that we have enclosures on our left. These continue for some distance then veer away to the north. We now have a marshy area below us and to the left of the track and beyond this White Barrow lies on our right. This large cairn is another prehistoric burial place and here we turn away from the track and walk nearly northwards along the contours, making for Lynch Tor which is in full view about a mile away. As we go we shall cross the line of a track coming up from our right which has forked off the one we left a short time ago. This is the Lich Path, here barely discernible, along which in medieval times the dead were brought for burial at Lydford from the farms and settlements in the Forest near Postbridge and Bellever.

We leave the Lich Path and cross Stooky Moor (Wapsworthy Common on the map) to Lynch Tor, passing Limsboro' (another cairn and Forest boundmark) en route. From the summit of Lynch Tor we can plainly see, less than a mile away to the NE, the great boulder strewn hill of Standon, which lies just across the valley of the Baggator Brook.

It is now time for us to steer for home. This we do by taking a course of about WSW from Lynch Tor, making for the low eminence of Baggator which we can see a trifle over a mile away with the little church of Brentor on its conical hilltop nearly four miles beyond that. About 300 yards below the summit of Lynch Tor we reach a shallow gully, running nearly due north and south at this point. This is the old peat path which formerly carried the carts laden with peat on their way from the Walkhamhead peat diggings which lie in the Walkham valley about a mile to the NE of Lynch Tor. We can if we like follow this old track, first south and then west and it will bring us quite soon into the wide stroll between the enclosures. The stroll gradually narrows as we proceed, getting more and more rutted as it does so. It seems pretty certain that we are now walking along the Lich Path again which merges with the peat track hereabouts. Further to the SE its route is uncertain until White Barrow is reached; there it joins the Peter Tavy track which we followed earlier and runs down to cross the Walkham at Sandy Ford.

The track we are following ends at Baggator Gate, just a few yards to the SW of the tor of the same name. The Lich Path used to go straight on, making for Cataloo Steps or Standon Steps, both on the River Tavy, according to the anticipated state of the river. But in the vicinity of Baggator Gate only a shallow gully can be seen which follows what was probably the line of the track. We pass through the moor gate into the lane beyond and walk west and SW along it for about three-quarters of a mile. We now see a finger post indicating a footpath on the right of the road, pointing to a short cantilevered flight of steps which gives access to the top of the wall. On the other side are more steps which bring us down into a grass field which we cross obliquely, taking a south-westerly course. Having crossed three fields in this fashion, the ground falling all the time towards the valley of the Tavy, we at last come to another stile which brings us out into the road at Hill bridge. As we cross the fields we are assisted by yellow or orange blobs of paint on the boulders, etc. marking the line of the path. The views of the river as we descend are very fine, especially those upstream.

Having reached the road we cross the bridge and make our way uphill to the gate of Hill Bridge Farm through which we came on the outward journey. From this point onwards the route is familiar to us and we reach our cars on Zoar Common after a walk of about a mile from Hill Bridge.

EXPLORATION 19. Cross Furzes, the Abbots' Way, Lambs' Down, Avon Reservoir, Redlake, Broad Falls, Huntingdon Warren.

(CLEAR OF ALL FIRING AREA)

Starting place:
Cross Furzes (near Buckfastleigh). Map reference 700666.

Approach:
From Exeter, Torquay, Newton Abbot, etc. via Buckfastleigh by way of the A38.
From Plymouth, as above.
From Tavistock, Okehampton, etc. via Two Bridges by way of B3375, turning off to Holne about 1 mile beyond New Bridge. Alternatively join A38 near Plymouth, turning off at Buckfastleigh.

Amenities:
All amenities at Buckfastleigh. Public toilets at Buckfast. Public house (Church House Inn), Post Office, shop and cafe at Holne.

Parking for the exploration:
There is limited parking at the starting place.

Type of excursion:
Easy moorland walking. A few steep climbs. About 10 miles which can be extended or curtailed at will.

This walk is somewhat longer than most excursions described in this book. Quite apart from its length, the walk is so packed with items of interest which the explorer will wish to examine that it is wise to set apart a whole day for its accomplishment. It should not be attempted by inexperienced walkers in any but a period of settled weather unless an experienced guide is available.

Cross Furzes is about 3 miles WNW of Buckfastleigh and a little over 2 miles south of Holne. 250 yards to the SSE of the point marked Cross Furzes on the map there is a T-junction (with Cross Furzes on the signpost) – or cross-roads if you count the rough track which runs steeply downhill to the south-west. This is the starting place for the expedition – the rough track being the commencement of the moorland section of the Abbots' Way. This ancient track is reputed to have been used by the monks of the three abbeys on the

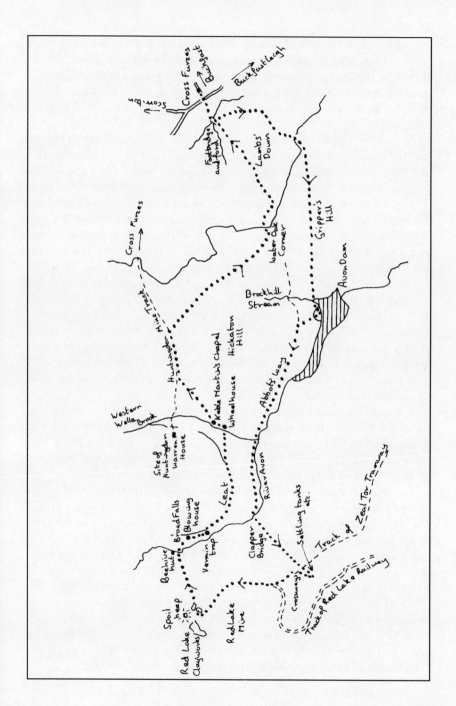

immediate perimeter of the Moor, i.e. Buckfast, Tavistock and Buckland, when visiting each other or when traversing the Moor for other purposes. Whilst there is little true evidence of this, there can be no doubt that the track had been used for centuries by people having business on and around the Moor, particularly in the days before the two main roads which now cross the Moor were constructed.

At first our path lies along this rough steep lane, and, after about 200 yards, we find ourselves at the bottom of the valley. Ahead of us is a little stream – the Dean Burn – spanned at this point by a clapper bridge consisting of two lengths of granite placed end to end. The bridge bears two dates – 1705 and 1737. One of the two stones was replaced in the 1960s having been missing for many years. Alongside the bridge is a fording place and beyond it a gate through which lies our path. Beyond the gate on the right, we find an ancient hedgebank with a number of very large beech trees growing in it, and here the track divides into two sections. Just beyond the trees there is a gap in the hedge bank; the Abbots' Way goes through this gap but our track veers away to the left and then begins to rise steeply. There is a signpost by the gate indicating the two tracks. Ours is the one marked "South Brent by way of Moor Cross". Our route at the moment is a well marked cart track, rough and sometimes muddy. It continues to rise for some distance but after about a quarter of a mile the land flattens out a little and we now see that we are walking through a large grassy enclosure with ancient walls and hedgebanks to our right where there are a number of very large beech trees.

A few minutes spent here examining the site and regaining our breath will be well repaid. The place we have arrived at was formerly the site of Lambs' Down Farm and no doubt the trees were planted to provide a windbreak. No trace of a building is now to be found and how long ago the farm was abandoned seems to be unknown; certainly not within living memory.

We continue along our track for a few more hundred yards, until it brings us to a gateway set in a rocky hollow. We pass through the gate and having gained the high ground beyond, look around us. We now find that we are on the open moor and that the track we have followed so far veers away sharply to the south-east. It is now time for us to leave this track and we turn to the west. Ahead of us the land still rises, but gently now, to reach the summit of Gripper's Hill about half a mile away and to this we make our way. On reaching the top and looking down into the valley beyond we see a sheet of water which culminates in a dam below us to the left but extends up the valley to the NW to a point beyond our view. This is the Avon Reservoir, constructed in the early 1950s by damming the valley of the River Avon. We have seen this dam from a different angle in our expedition from Shipley Bridge.

From the summit of Gripper's Hill we make our way downhill almost due west so as to strike the reservoir at a point where a tiny stream falls into the lake. The stream is the Brockhill Stream and having reached it we cross to the further side by means of the many rocks lying in its bed. We then walk along the edge of the reservoir with the water on our left until we come to what is clearly a tumbledown wall. On passing through the wall we find that we are in an enclosure, partly surrounded by the wall and partly by the water of the lake – the wall in fact disappears under the water at both ends. The enclosure covers about two and a half acres and contains a dozen or more Bronze Age huts or, as they are now called, hut circles.

When it was decided to flood this valley to make the reservoir the prehistoric village here was exhaustively examined by archaeologists and many interesting facts came to light, including evidence that the inhabitants of the village had used metal tools in their daily life. Unexpectedly, it was found that the prehistoric enclosure had been extended in medieval times and a farmstead constructed here by the monks of Buckfast Abbey. The two rectangular buildings which formed this farmstead are now under the water of the reservoir but can still be seen in a very dry summer such as we experienced in 1976. The archaeologists were able to tentatively date the prehistoric occupation of this site as having extended into late Bronze Age times, probably in the vicinity of 800 B.C.

Having completed our investigation of the prehistoric village we turn to the NW and make our way up the sloping hillside for about 300 yards. We now strike a well marked track, sometimes muddy, sometimes stony, which runs from east to west above the reservoir. This is the Abbots' Way which we left not far from Cross Furzes on setting out on our excursion. To reach this ancient track we cross the line of a post and wire fence, now happily dismantled, which surrounded the reservoir from the date of its construction until early in 1981 when it was removed. A word of caution here; although public access to the reservoir is unrestricted this is an act of grace on the part of the Water Authority and not because of the existence of a public right. But bathing is not permitted, nor is fishing without a permit and the water is deep and may be dangerous to children, so ...

We now turn to the left and walk more or less westward along the Abbots' Way. At the moment we have high rising ground on our right and on our left and below us the waters of the reservoir. Beyond the lake the land rises steeply for about half a mile to reach a narrow plateau which extends to the west and north-west for another mile before it begins to slope down again into the valley of the River Erme some two and a half miles away. We shall see more of this part of the world a little later on. At the moment we find that as we proceed the reservoir below us is getting narrower and narrower until it eventually tapers off and becomes a mere stream, the River Avon.

At a point about half a mile from where we struck it, the Abbots' Way brings us to the banks of another small stream – the Western Wella Brook – coming down from the north to join the Avon. We cross the little tributary at a ford or on the rocks nearby and then notice, ahead of us and quite close, a ruined stone wall and a stone cross. The cross is Huntingdon Cross and the wall encloses the 600 acres or so which formerly comprised Huntingdon Warren, which lies on both sides of the Avon for well over a mile. The cross was erected about 1550 to mark the bounds of the Manor of Brent following the Dissolution of the Monasteries when the land belonging to Buckfast Abbey came into private hands.

Huntingdon Cross

Another such cross, Petre's Cross, can still be seen in a mutilated condition standing on Western White Barrow nearly a mile away to the SW. Huntingdon Warren lies within the Forest of Dartmoor (the Western Wella Brook is the boundary) and it seems to have come into existence about 1800. Here rabbits were farmed as a crop and this industry continued until the 1920s, we are told.

Close by Huntingdon Cross is a somewhat dubious ford and here originally the Abbots' Way crossed the river. We do not do so however but continue upstream with the river on our left. The best path lies not along the river bank but a little distance from it. After about half a mile we reach a spot from which we can see, ahead of us and spanning the river, a clapper bridge constructed from slabs of rock of great size. This bridge is said to have been built by one of the warreners at Huntingdon so that he might have easy access to his territory on the south side of the river. It seems to have given him some trouble however, as it was used by claydiggers and peatcutters who lived at their workings on the south side of the river to cross the stream to poach the warrener's rabbits.

Huntingdon Clapper Bridge

We now cross the river, but before doing so we take stock of our surroundings. Upstream and on either side we are closed in by high rising ground with the river flowing towards us through a narrow defile. Downstream however the view is different – in this direction the valley opens out and we can see part of the hillside of Huntingdon Warren and east of that Hickaton Hill.

At the foot of the latter, only a couple of hundred yards from the river but unseen to those who pass below it, is a splendid enclosure with a number of hut circles adjacent to it. Perhaps we should have stopped to examine it since we came so close; but then, we have already explored one such and this part of the Moor contains so many examples of this kind of monument that it would be impossible to examine them all. There are others within view on the lower slopes of Huntingdon Warren and we can always come back again another day.

From the clapper bridge we now face a stiff climb of about 300 yards up the hillside to the SW. There is a quite well marked path and as we rise the valley below opens out and gives views of southern Dartmoor so far not seen. Soon we pass through a ruined wall and now the gradient is becoming less steep until, when we are about 700 yards from the bridge, we emerge upon a plateau extending NW and SE for a considerable distance. We continue our south-westerly course and notice that the character of the ground has now changed. We are still on rough grassy moorland but frequently we see large rectangular areas lying below the general level of the ground.

These are peat-ties, areas from which the peat has been removed in times past and taken for processing at the peatworks at Shipley Bridge about three miles away to the SW. We also come across long shallow gullies which are all that remain of the Zeal Tor Tramway which carried the peat to Shipley. We also see one or two small ruined buildings connected with the peat industry.

A little further on we reach a large collection of filter-beds, mica traps, settling pits and other remains of the china clay workings which also existed here in the 19th century. These will inevitably take some time to examine but

Settling tanks –
Crossways

then we turn away to the north. As we do so we notice something that has so far not been commented upon. This is a large conical pile of material presenting a blackish-whitish streaked appearance as it stands upon the skyline to the north nearly a mile away. We make a bee-line for this across the open moor and soon come upon what is plainly the line of yet another tramway.

Spoil heap at Red Lake

This is the Redlake tramway and following it we find that it is bringing us nearer and nearer to the conical heap. Soon the tramway is joined by another coming in from the south and then we see that on either side of us are numerous deep but narrow trenches – more peat-ties in fact – from which the peat was taken to be loaded on to the tramway trucks. Now the tramway begins to veer away to the NW and a quarter of a mile further on we reach our objective – the spoil-heaps and flooded workings of the Redlake China Clay Works.

Here, in one of the most desolate areas of southern Dartmoor the Redlake China Clay Works was established in 1910. It was connected with the diggings at Leftlake just over two miles to the south and with the drying plant at Cantrell, over seven miles away, by a railway – the Redlake Mineral Railway – along the track of which we have just walked. It is said that at the height of the industry about 100 men were employed here. They lived "on the job" and it was they, so it is said, who poached the rabbits belonging to the warrener at Huntingdon. The industry closed down in 1932 because of difficulties experienced in separating the base elements from the china clay proper and because the pits were becoming worked out.

The spoil heap at Redlake is a landmark for miles around; there are three ponds, one large and two smaller ones, which are of course the flooded areas from which the clay had been taken. Some strange ornithological visitors arrive here from time to time. I remember seeing both shag and Canada geese disporting themselves at Redlake at one time or another.

We have now reached the turning point in our expedition, so we turn to the

NE and follow the path which runs between the two smaller ponds. After about 700 yards of open moorland this brings us back to the River Avon again, which we strike at Broad Falls. Here the river, having made a sharp turn from SW to SE, rapidly loses height. The area, including the river bed, is very rocky hence the name of the place.

There is no great difficulty in crossing the river on the many rocks but before doing so a search on the level ground just above the western bank in the vicinity of the falls may bring to light another curiosity in the shape of a small domed building – ruinous it is true but unmistakably the remains of one of the many bee-hive huts formerly to be found on Dartmoor. These huts are thought to have been tinners' caches where the old miners hid their untaxed ingots or whatever other valuables they may have had.

Having crossed the river we remain on the high ground above the stream until we have cleared the area of the falls, then we descend to river level. Almost immediately we see ahead of us and quite close to the river a small ruined building. This is a blowing house, i.e. a place where tin ore was crushed and smelted in ancient times. How old this building is is unknown, but it may well be of 17th century date. It is very ruinous but the site of the wheelpit which housed the water-wheel can still be identified as can the furnace and the leat which brought the water to the wheel. Lying on the grass between the building and the river is a block of granite with two saucer shaped depressions in it. This was the mortar in which the ore was crushed prior to smelting.

On leaving the blowing house we continue to walk along the river bank for another quarter of a mile or so. Then we come to a spot where the path narrows to a few inches and in fact runs between two adjacent slabs of rock lying parallel with the river and with each other. Stop and look! It will be found that the inner faces of these slabs are equipped with grooves as though to accommodate a slide or shutter. This is indeed the case for what we have found are the remains of a vermin trap, used by the warreners of the 18th century or earlier to catch the stoats and weasels which preyed upon their rabbits. This specimen is unfortunately incomplete; originally it would have been fitted with a lid and with slate shutters which ran in the grooves and which would be actuated by a pressure plate and spring mechanism. There are dozens of these old traps to be found near Dartmoor's disused warrens if only one knows how to identify them.

It is now time to leave the river bank and so we strike in a north-easterly direction up the steep hillside until we come to the dry channel of an old leat. We follow this channel as it contours the hillside. It passes close by the upper edge of two prehistoric enclosures containing hut circles and then begins to veer towards the north. If we stop at this point we shall see below us, about a couple of hundred yards away in the direction of the river, a dark area with what appears to be a small building adjoining it. This is worth investigation and when we get to it we find that we are looking at a badly depleted hut circle with a small roofless shelter close to it.

Wester Wella Brook

There are two or three such shelters on the hillside and it seems likely that the old warrener built them for his own purposes – perhaps to enable him to observe the activities of poachers in comfort. There is no need to return to the dry leat; instead we take a north-easterly course, making for the valley of the Western Wella Brook which we can see coursing down the hillside about 300 yards away. On reaching the stream we cross as close as possible to a building that we have already observed on the further side. This turns out to be a long, narrow and, as usual, roofless building which formerly housed a large water-wheel which was used to pump out the mine working at the New Huntingdon Tin Mine which was re-opened in 1864 on the site of a much older mine. The mine workings lie all around and cover a considerable area though it seems that the mine was never very prosperous.

Quite close to the old wheel-pit but nearer the stream and a little to the north is another item of interest. This is always known locally as Keble Martin's Chapel (or Church). It consists of a small roofless building with one rounded end reminiscent of the apse of a church. At the other (northern) end is a raised flat slab bearing a short pillar of granite upon which is carved a small cross.

The building gives the impression of never having had a roof. The story is that Keble Martin, later a well known Devon clergyman and famous for his authorship of *The Concise British Flora in Colour,* used to camp here as a young man together with his brother and their friends. It is on record that on one occasion they baptised a baby, the child of the warrener at Huntingdon, and also that they ate largely of rabbit pies made by the warrener's wife.

Keble Martin's Chapel

We now turn away from the stream and make our way NE across the rough open moor for about a quarter of a mile. For most of this distance we shall be walking among old mine workings which consist mostly of pits and gullies, with one or two deepish shafts which could be quite dangerous if not treated with respect. Soon however we strike a well marked track coming up from the east and making for the warren house and farm. If we stand here for a moment we shall be struck by the beauty of the distant scenery which extends over a wide area to the east and north. We shall also see behind us to the west the nearby hillside of Huntingdon Warren with the site of the house and farm beyond the stream we have just left. The house has long since been pulled down, though it was still standing in the 1950s, but its position is clear for all to see, as are the tiny paddocks and little fields and the many artificial rabbit burrows that lie all around.

Our path now lies to the east, along the track we have just reached and we follow this over the pleasant springy turf for a quarter of a mile or a little more. We then reach a spot where our track is intersected by another running from SE to NW. We turn right-handed into this path and make our way across the undulating moorland for almost a mile, until we reach a spot known as Water Oak Corner. There is no mistaking this place, which is within view long before we actually reach it, as it is marked by a windswept copse of pine trees standing in the angle of two walls at the spot where the enclosures to the east meet the open moorland to the south, west and north. There is a small gateway in the wall close to the trees and going through this we follow the path, first to the east and then south-east across Lambs' Down.

We are now on the Abbots' Way again and ahead of us, almost a mile away, we can see Cross Furzes and can even discern our cars standing on the edge of the common. Soon the land begins to fall quite steeply and then we reach the hedgebank with the great beech trees that we saw at the very beginning of our excursion. We pass through a gap in the hedgebank and there ahead of us is the gate giving access to the little clapper bridge over the Dean Burn and the rugged lane beyond at the head of which are our cars.

Gorse